# THE
# MISSING MOON

## AND OTHER CASE STUDIES

from the files of
MICHAEL MERCURY, ASTROLOGER

by
NOEL TYL

A Short-Story Reader in Astrology

**First Edition 1979**
Second Printing, 2015

Llewellyn Publications
2143 Wooddale Drive
Woodbury, Minnesota 55125-2989

International Standard Book Number: 978-0-7387-4718-7

*Printed in the United States of America*

All similarities to people extraordinary,
to biographical and astrological accuracy
are interestingly coincidental.

to those astrologers who,
through these fantasies and exaggeration,
may with me
appreciate more
the mysterious truths that fill our lives

# CONTENTS

"*Mr. Yuga has come!*"

## Chapter One

## *THE CASE OF THE MISSING MOON*

Christmas was coming. I didn't have to check the ephemeris to be sure: the Salvation Army was already playing for contributions in front of Bloomingdale's. —what brass they had! So much agony in the world and in my office five floors above it, and *they* played with cheer. Sure, they want to create the giving spirit and collect for the needy. They're effective. Maybe they should do it all year 'round. I do. I'm up here all the time, giving everything I've got to the most unusual clients in the world. What if *I* greeted my clients with a trombone in my hand! Wouldn't that be something! But really, astrology *is* salvation to people, and I guess I'm a one-man army.

"Cally! . . . Cally, orbit in here for a minute, will you!"

'Cally' . . . short for 'Callisto.' Some name. I couldn't believe it: the employment agency sending me a secretary applicant with the name of one of Jupiter's satellites! Zeus' wife caught her and turned her into a bear. I have days like that, too!

"Cally . . . "

"Easy does it, Merk. I got retrograded for a minute. What's up?"

"Have you drawn up that horoscope for the 2 o'clock? He'll be here in about 40 minutes, and I want to look it over."

"Yep. Here. It's a doozy!"

She handed me the horoscope: 'Male, February 29, 1930, Oradea, Rumania; Aries Ascendant, Sun-Venus in the XIIth in Pisces, opposing Neptune'. . . . Mmmmm. This will be interesting indeed.

"You're sure there aren't any mistakes, Cally? You checked everything carefully? You may be gal 'Thursday,' but sometimes you don't have your Mercury in gear right after lunch!" I teased.

"Merk! Look who's talking. You're so nervous today. You're the Mercury that's not in the right gear. And anyway, I worked on it after coffee-break this morning while you were talking with Paula Pergator. Wha. is with her anyway? Big Italian actress with all her goodies?"

"That's none of your business, Cal. You know I can't discuss certain problems with you. I have taken the Astrology Association's Hypocyclic Oath, and 'ethics' is the thing with me . . . THE thing. That's why we're so successful! I've got the goodies and I'm ethical, and that's why we have the most fascinating clients in the world. We do it with astrology, pure and simple. I wouldn't get anywhere playing 'Silent Night' for them, would I?"

"Easy does it, Merk. I was just curious. But I've put a few charts together where the Star of Bethlehem could have helped matters!"

"Sorry, Cally. I'm all keyed up. I've got a feeling something really important is going to happen soon. Today one of the asteroids ringing Vulcan is in a progressed parallel of declination with my South Node of Uranus conjunct my Ascendant . . . and there's a quincunx between transiting Mars and my Part of Expectation!"

"Want some coffee?"

"No, thanks. Let me have some quiet now. I've got to get ready for 2 o'clock. No name this time, huh?"

"Nope. This one's mysterious. Please check it and call if you want anything." She said that strangely.

"Thanks. Close the door, please."

My gosh! Look at that horoscope! Leap-year birth. And the guy knew his birth-time down to the second! Can that be true?

"Cally! CALLY!"

"What's wrong?"

"Did this man really give his time in seconds . . . or did you fudge around with it?"

"No, honest, Merk. He said it loud and clear . . . with a heavy accent and a voi—"

"Yes, he was born in Rumania."

"And his voice was so deep. Like a classical actor. I didn't touch the horoscope. And I really doublechecked the Standard Time Meridian: some sources say Rumania was on 30 East after 1891. Other sources say not until 1931. And before that, in 1930, when he was born, they worked with Bucharest at 26 East. I did it for 30. It's right . . . I really worked carefully. But please, *you* check it."

"OK. Thanks."

*Me* check it—she's sure, yet not so sure. Fascinating. He's really got something here: Sun-Venus conjunction in the XIIth in Pisces, intercepted, opposing Neptune. . . maybe he's living in some idealized dream. Wow! There's the 'Roosevelt' Uranus rising. . . but in Aries. . . and the 'Hitler-Napoleon' Saturn at the Midheaven, in Capricorn; what a square! And Jupiter is square the Sun-Venus/Neptune axis. That's a T-Square discharging into the VIIIth-IXth region. Maybe this guy's making money with his fantasy in foreign countries. . . and then the trine to Pluto.

"Cally, CAL-LY!" Where in the world is this man's Moon? For Pete's sake, can't you check your work? What in the Heaven do you—"

"I know, Merk. I'm scared to death: the mood you're in, I didn't. . . couldn't tell you. . . Uh, I was hoping you'd check the ephemeris for yourself and you'd see it was a New Moon day. . . but. . . but the Moon simply *is not* listed in the ephemeris. . . and there's no errata note. . . and the day before and the day after measure normal Moon movement. I don't know wha—"

"What? Get me the ephemeris. . ."

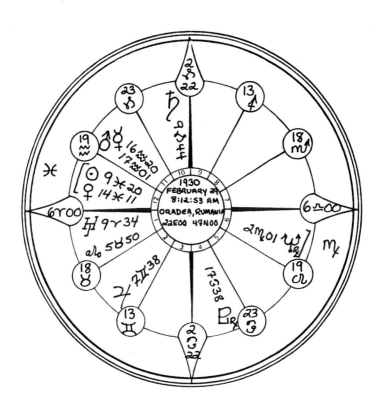

1930, August, April, March, February. . . 27, 28, 29.
*No Moon*. NO MOON! No note. . . normal the next day. . .
but here none! "Cally, you're right! But there must be
a Moon position. . . the motions before and after check
out. What can we do?"

All I could hear was "It Came Upon a Midnight Clear."
*I* was anything *but* clear. Only 20 minutes to go and Mr.
Rumania would be here.

"I'll call Mr. Clyptic. . . maybe he'll have an explanation."

My palms were wet. Never in the history of Astrology
had this happened. A man without a Moon! Holy Smokes!
What can it mean. . . what can it mean? I dialed the phone.

"Mr. Clyptic. Michael Mercury. Sorry to interrupt,
but I've got a question. I've *really* got a question for you."

I explained the situation. Clyptic had been a great
teacher. . . still was. Smoke came out of his ears when he
got going with the mystery stuff. Smoke practically came
out of the phone with his guarded answer:

"Merk, I never cover this in my classes. And I've never
had anyone bring this date to my attention. But I do know
about it. I learned about this date from Friederich von
Finsternis when I studied with him in Heidelberg in '26.
He told me the date would occur in 1930."

"But how did *he* know it was going to occur? Had
it happened before? Why have I never heard or read anything about it?" I questioned frantically.

Clyptic continued slowly: "Von Finsternis had
studied with a Russian seer years before, 1865 or so I
think, in Cairo, and this man had spent his lifetime study-

ing the Sanskrit texts, Atlantean references in Herotodus and other works, and alchemy scrolls discovered in the Pyramids. This man had discovered that the Moon actually disappeared ev—"

"Disappeared???" I shouted.

"Yes, disappeared every 2,160 years in close synchronization with Sign shifts in the Precession of Equinoxes."

I whistled into the phone. "But why, how can that happen?"

"That's why this is dangerous information, Merk."

"What do you mean? I've got this man coming in here, and he was *born* on that day. . . of ALL days. . . and I can't talk about his Moon. *Every* astrologer has to talk about the Moon!"

"I know. I know. I guess I must tell you. But this is strange lore, Merk. You've got to be careful."

"I'm already having one hell of a strange day, Mr. Clyptic. Nothing can upset me now. Please: I'll stop talking; I've got to have an explanation, *the* explanation."

"Alright," he paused. "Merk, remember in the Bible that it refers to the Sun standing still; Joshua prayed for a long day to win a battle, and the Sun did stand still?"

"I know. And that scientist, Veli-something-or-other, the Russian, checked cultures on the other side of the Earth and found that the *Moon* had stood still at the same time. The story checked out throughout religions and legends."

"Correct, Merk. And, of course, geologists know that that was a cataclysmic time for the earth: stopping and restarting, etc. I'll skip those details since I know you're rushed."

"Thanks. I am. He'll be here any minute. Excuse me . . . Cally, better go out and wait at your desk. Buzz me as soon as he comes. OK, Mr. Clyptic. Sorry for the interruption."

"Well, the analysis of all those ancient works showed that, as the Sun changes Signs during the grand Precession cycle, the Moon would transcendentally disappear for one day at each of the twelve cusp points."

"What? 'Transcendentally'? But, Mr. Clyptic, we're *scientists*."

"Yes, we are. But we're also transcendental communicators. We communicate mysteries in a scientific form. The science gives us security and practical uniformity. But the transcendental must enter our awareness, the awareness of the universe in every new epoch in the Precession cycle."

"Say that again, please."

"The Moon disappears so that special grand illumination, the fecundation of an Age can come to earth *directly* from the Sun. . . not reflected or given form by the Moon. . . . directly from the Sun into the Earth's awareness. It's a kind of heavenly genuflection before the Sun as it moves into a new mode."

I could practically see the smoke coming out of Clyptic's ears. Wow!

"So, cryptically speaking, Mr. Clyptic, it's a heavenly acknowledgment of some new gift from the Sun. Right?"

"Correct."

"And who gathers up the direct illumination? The whole world?"

"Yes, the whole world. But von Finsternis claimed that his Russian teacher said it was focused upon one or more very special individuals throughout the world, and these individuals would become the womb of world-changing thought and discovery."

"You mean an initiate into the mysteries, like Newton?"

"An initiate, yes."

"But why haven't science, astronomy, even just ordinary people missed seeing the Moon on that day?"

"That's very difficult to answer, Merk. Such a highly sensitive time is also a very frightening time. It comes only once every 2,160 years. Science is afraid to question the phenomenon. People assume the Moon is where they can't see it, or that it's too cloudy. Science looks at the situation similarly. To make a big expose' really would serve no purpose. There's no real precedent on how to handle it. It's better left ignored. After all, it's only a small computation during one day in two millennia, and the Moon is always there the next day."

"But the other positions are in the Ephemeris. . . with the Moon left out. And what happens to people born on that day?"

"*No one* is ever born on that day, Merk."

"WHAAAT???"

"No one is ever born on that day according to the ancient sources. It is a day of transcendental fecundation . . . and, as always with the impregnation of the spirit, a certain blindness occurs as well."

"I'm beginning to see, Mr. Clyptic."

"The day occurs in the ephemeris, because the Astrolo Brotherhood knows this lore too. They give reverence to the day. And astrologers somehow, some way, come to this date in experience or study and seek out the explanation the way you have. Some get to understand; others don't."

"But Mr. Clyptic, I HAVE a client who *was* born on this day. He's probably coming up in the elevator right now! He knows his birth to the second . . . 8:12:53!!"

"Merk, you are part of the mystery today. Does your horoscope show special conditions for today?"

"It sure does: Vulcan asteroid in progressed parallel with my Uranus South Node and . . ."

This time it was Clyptic who whistled in surprise! "Please, Merk, call me here or at home as soon as you're through. And Merk, be careful, you're in touch with a mystery."

"Yes, sir, thank you. I'll call."

As soon as I had put down the telephone, Cally's buzzer sounded. He's here. I had shivers. I was frightened. I felt weak and strong at the same time. I wasn't out of control, but I felt I needed help somehow.

"Yes, Cally? He's here?"

"Yes, yes, he's . . ."

Her voice sounded empty, hushed. I dismissed her, hanging up the phone, and went immediately to my office door.

He was standing in the doorway. As soon as I opened the door, there he was, like a materialization. He stood so still. In that second of meeting, my eyes took in as much as possible: he was dressed completely in black, a long opera cape over his shoulders, tied across his chest. Only his hands showed through slits in the cape. They hung at his side absolutely motionless, as if weighted by lead cuff-links. That would be his Saturn. And then his face: pleasant, healthy, a little red-swarthy, slightly pointed chin . . . and the eyes . . . the pattern of blood vessels in the right eye especially . . . these things told me . . . corroborated the Aries Ascendant perfectly. The forehead had the Uranian bulge. I remembered that picture in Lucellan Scorpio's textbook! The man smiled pleasantly. There was nothing Mephistophelean about him. The black was comforting in a way. He was obviously so well tailored, so perfectly groomed. This moment of awareness was broken by my, "Good afternoon; please come in. I'm Michael Mercury."

He glided, wafted into the room without a word and stood before my desk. He obviously was waiting for me to take my place behind it. I motioned for him to sit, did so myself, the suspended awareness of identity intriguing me, calling my professional powers of observation into action, displacing some of the panicky bewilderment I had felt only moments before. His eyes were soft, kind, far-away, yet all-encompassing. There was Sun-Venus in Pisces with the Neptune opposition.

The tension in the room was really over who would speak first. He seemed to cooperate with my studying him, enjoyed it perhaps . . . that emphasis of the ego from the eastern organization of planets. Just as I began to speak, he seized the initiative:

"Mr. Merkurius, I have come."

That's all. He said simply 'I have come,' but he said it like a Greek actor delivering a Delphic message.

"I'm happy to see you, sir. Thank you for being on time. May I please know your name?"

"My name is Yuga."

"Yuga. Mr. Yuga, you speak with no accent at all! My secretary said . . ."

"I am a man of many accents, many worlds."

For *him* to say these words, there was no strangeness at all. I believed him or whatever he meant, easily.

"Mr. Yuga, I've done your horoscope, but before we talk about it, may I ask you why you want to have it done?"

"I have it done at intervals," he intoned, "to measure my progress."

"Fine. You *were* born in Oradea, Rumania, February 29, 1930, at 8:12:53 in the morning?"

"Yes."

"How do you know the time so exactly?"

"I knew when I was coming."

"From a previous life?"

"Yes."

"Well, your horoscope *is* exceptional and there are indications of super-normal sensitivity which could . . ."

"Mr. Merkurius, let's get to the point." he interrupted genially.

"The point?"

"The irregularity." he said.

"The irregularity?"

"The irregularity."

"Mr. Yuga, your horoscope shows no Moon. It sounds strange, it's impossible, yet it seems that there is precedent." I was becoming hesitant. "I've heard that —no, first let me ask you: have you ever met anyone else born on this same day?"

"In a way, yes."

"In a way?"

"In a way. But please," he soothed, "I know something about astrology. May I suggest that we discuss the horoscope *without* the Moon."

"Without the Moon! But that's the key to the personality, Mr. Yuga. I *have* to discuss it . . . "

"No you don't," he interrupted again. "I was born at New Moon. One never sees the Moon at New Moon."

"You're right, but we know it's there." We seemed to have agreed on a crucial point. "But on this day it *wasn't* there!"

"Now *you* sound strange!" he said with a smile.

"Yes I do . . . but . . . well, you know so much: *was* it there?"

"It was very new."

"I must laugh, Mr. Yuga: being a New Moon is absolute —being *very* new is an impossibility . . . like . . . like being a 'little bit' pregnant. One *is* or *isn't*."

"Precisely."

"Precisely?" I questioned.

"Precisely: becoming pregnant. One cannot 'see' the moment, the process, the instant of seeding."

"I see." Again we were agreeing strangely, "There *was* something very special, very new about this New Moon."

"Fine. Now we're getting somewhere." Yuga seemed to be controlling the interview, definitely.

"But you've made this appointment with me —what can I, should I do for you?"

"Read my horoscope . . . "

"Without the Moon," we said simultaneously.

We were both relaxing now. I could imagine Cally outside, frightened. After all, she had made the discovery and was scared to death. I could imagine Clyptic waiting to hear back from me . . . all the astrologers of the world. What a man sat before me! What a horoscope! I've done some beauts in my practice, but so often eccentricity was problematic, off-beat, disruptive somehow. With this man, the unusual had such depth, such dignity. I felt strangely part of it all. He pulled his arm into and under his cape and loosened the black velvet clasp at the collar. The cape fell back onto the chair. His suit was beautiful black silk. Not like a cardinal's or priest's. More like a billionaire with eccentric tastes, a man with the riches of the world somehow contrasted by elegant austerity. He had no tie: his shirt was strange. It was a kind of pleated turtle-neck in soft gray. It almost shimmered with the silver of silk weaving. A medallion hung around his neck, like a military decoration: it was an emblem of Uranus.

"Alright, Mr. Yuga, let me tell you what I see, but please, please don't let me go on if I sound foolish to you, please. I'll do my best." I felt shocked into another Self.

I began: "The Sun in conjunction with Venus in Pisces is opposing Neptune. Often this is a debilitating factor in a horoscope, especially with the Sun and Venus in the XIIth House, especially if the Moon . . . Excuse me. Here, I would have to suggest that the fantasy is . . . uh, a measure of the tran-scen-den-tal in your personality." These last words I said so slowly, remembering Mr. Clyptic.

I continued, "The rising Uranus in the Aries ascendant: this is a potential of genius, Mr. Yuga—and the Midheaven Saturn squaring Uranus . . . well, a whole generation would be born under this square, but on *your* birthday . . . and the aspect is exact then . . . time, ambition, Saturn and genius innovation, perhaps electrified potential, buckle together. The old, the established, is forced to give way to the new, and if the Moon were . . . uh . . . the Mars-Mercury conjunction in Aquarius in the XIth would echo the Uranian image, wouldn't they? Your dreams, your hopes and wishes for man, well, they could be Utopian, couldn't they, remembering the Sun-Venus-Neptune configurations? Jupiter in Gemini squares the fantasy, the transcendental dimension. This is a T-square, discharged into Sagittarius in the VIIIth and IXth, ruled by Jupiter. This would mean that these higher mind faculties you have have considerable expansive thrust and communication structure. Pluto trines the Sun-Venus, sextiles Neptune . . . that would be a grand projection of your energies, your sensitivity, your home . . . uh, your position with man on Earth . . . a new beginning." Again these words sounded strange to me; I was reading the aspects at the highest level possible. I noted quickly that Pluto had just been discovered by man January 20, 1930, forty days before Yuga's birth . . . it was opposed by Mars at discovery, and the Sun had just entered Aquarius. His Sun was in Pisces, to progress into Aries, a whole new cycle.

"The orientation of all the bodies, except Neptune

and Pluto, to the East," I continued, "Usually emphasize the Ego. But here perhaps it emphasizes the personal gifts you have. The challenge of the life would be to give, to communicate, to share your being, your birth . . . " My words trailed off. Mr. Yuga smiled.

"Very good, Mr. Merkurius. Very good indeed. You're more of an astrologer than I even expected."

"Thank you, sir." That was all I could say. I was practically floating, suspended in feeling and movement.

"Now please tell me about the transits at this time . . . and the Progressions, should they be relevant."

Under the glass cover of my desk, I had the transits of several decades noted, by the month. It was easy to note them during interviews. "Mr. Yuga, right now in early December 1969, Uranus has just crossed your VIIth cusp: this is usually a new beginning, rather unusual, strong with the public. Here, your individual 'gift' would some- how be given a significant start, new beginning with others. Saturn is conjunct your missing Moon's node . . . surely significant. Mars is conjunct the birth position of Mars. To sum it up quickly, a new cycle of promotion, self-promo- tion has begun. It would seem that your progress now is sharply fulfilled . . . the challenge of sharing; transcenden- tal illumination, if you will, is dramatically shared with others." I was suddenly proud of myself. All this was extraordinary.

"In a few days," I went on, "there will be a New Moon at 17 Sagittarius, involving your IXth House, the Sun-Venus conjunction, by square, also Mars-Mercury . . . and Pluto. This is a vital time indeed, Mr. Yuga." I paused and progressed the Sun quickly: "And your Sun, your Sun . . . you're almost to your 40th birthday: your Sun has Progressed to square with your birth Pluto!" I could hardly believe all this. Every aspect corroborated every other aspect.

"Excellent, Mr. Merkurius. No need to go further. If you were now to compute the progressed Moon, you'd see it was near an opposition . . . an awareness of my Mars-Mercury. It always *is* at times like this."

"Thank you, thank you . . . but I don't know if all this has answered your questions . . . about . . . about . . . your 'Progress', was that it? All indications speak of a very significant, unusual 'giving' at this time, a new cycle. Almost all vital points in your horoscope are activated. And this phenomenal Saturn in Capricorn: your ambition . . . your profession . . . your 'time' has come, I need your corrobora . . ."

"Please let me interrupt, Mr. Merkurius. You've pleased me. You are accurate. You have read my horoscope at a flattering high level. Indeed, I *am* sharing significantly what I have . . . *we* have met today." He paused without taking his eyes off me, then resumed: "I have no profession, no real ambition as you call it . . . as you must refer to it. But to be certain, the time has come for me: my time, your time, our time. The XIIth House, the XIIth Sign has been vacated. From one point of view, we are going into one direction, from another point of view we are going into another direction. The dynamism of change is what concerns me. Giving is the challenge in my horoscope, Mr. Merkurius. Man must look inside himself now to find that special something. It's his only salvation. And please, the missing Moon: don't let that concern you. Only the sensitive will be aware of it. New inspiration is born unseen. Time gives it form."

Then, most abruptly, he rose, fixed his cape, almost bowed and said, formally yet warmly: "I thank you for receiving me. I will mail you ·a check for your service. Fare-well."

His last word was curiously hyphenated. He turned gracefully, opened the door for himself and was into the hall before I could assist him. I followed him out past Cally's desk. She was frozen at her typewriter. He went through the second door without a sound or glance back.

"Cally," I whispered, "please ... what time is it now?"

"It's 10 minutes to three, 2:48."

"Please draw a chart for this moment."

"Wh-why?"

"It's my new birthday."

*"I've dispensed with the planets!"*

## Chapter Two

*THE CASE OF THE PARTILE PERSONALITY*

"Yes, Cally?"

Her voice was cheerful on the phone: "A Miss Bonnina Fortunata is calling."

"Bonnina Fortunata? Where do we get these names, Cally . . . Miss *Callisto*? We must be magnets for the unusual. OK, I'll take it; thanks."

I switched from intercom to line # 1. "Mercury speaking."

"Oh, Mr. Mercury, thank goodness I've reached you. I *must* see you as soon as possible. I feel I'm just falling apart."

"What's wrong, Miss Fortunata?"

"I was at your last lecture at Town Hall, and everything you said made such sense. I just *know* you can help me."

"Thank you, but what is wrong?"

Miss Fortunata went on and on about her 'falling apart.' We arranged a time the next morning at 9:00. She said I didn't have to draw her chart; she had done it, knew a great deal about astrology . . . enough to have appreciated my lecture series, and would save me the trouble by bringing her own chart with her. That was unusual, but a relief; I had a busy afternoon ahead of me.

Miss Fortunata arrived right on time. She was pleasant looking, a little overweight in an Italian way, strong face, strong hair, and a very real pride in her manner . . . probably a Leo Ascendant, and her clothes were all earth colors, with accents of bright orange and turquoise in her jewelry . . . probably a Taurus. She wore glasses, thick ones, which didn't detract at all from her ample good looks . . . but probably corroborated a stress aspect to Sun or Moon. She was about 34-35; Saturn would be squaring its birth position . . . the Saturn would have been in Pisces if she were really 34, and now, in Spring 1971, right upon her Sun, if she were really a Taurus. It is amazing what one can do in a glance. These first impressions are so often valid. She would have been born around 10 or 11 AM to get the Leo Ascendant, XIth House Sun.

We talked a bit . . . . really, *she* did all the talking: she was so organized in all her emotion. She seemed to be building up to something important. Then I saw what it was.

"So here's my horoscope, Mr. Mercury. I *do* know what I'm doing, and it will take some explaining. That's why I wanted to save you the trouble . . . why I drew it myself. Here."

She handed me the horoscope. I was flabbergasted!

"Miss Fortunata, what IS this? There aren't any planets at all? What are all these symbols?"

"They're Parts. I've drawn 21 Parts instead of the planetary positions in order to really structure the *nuance*, the prcper *synthesis* of my chart. I've worked with these Parts so long, I've *forgotten* where the planets are!"

"But *are* you a Taurus?" From her structuring she *had* to be.

"Yes . . . but you'll note that the Part of Life synthesis would indicate this by its posi—"

"And would you say that you had a Leo Ascendant. . . oh, yes, that *is* here."

"Yes, I was born at 10:35 in the morning here in New York City, but the Part of Spirit synthesizes this and, as you can see, it is finding maturity in its progressed position in the . . ."

"Miss Fortunata, please, give me a moment to appreciate what this is all about. First, I trust you corrected for Daylight Saving Time. May 17, 1937 *was* DST." She nodded. "But you have *dispensed* with the planets after having computed all these Parts? You believe that the synthesis is more valid because the birth positions have more dynamic relationships?"

"Yes. I *knew* you'd understand, Mr. Mercury, I just knew *you* would." She was jubilant, and her smile lit the room.

"But TWENTY-ONE PARTS !!!"

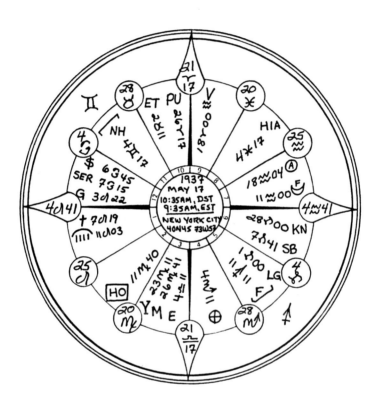

"Yes, the Part of Life—and I went back to Origannus to check that one out—the Part of Understanding, the Part of Brethren, the Part of Discord and Controversy, the Part of Journies by Water, the Part of Honorable and Illustrious Acquaintance—that's the Ascendant plus the Sun minus the Part of Fortune, which brings in the Moon, of course. . . beautiful. . . . the Part of Surgery. . . . "

She went on and on. Her mood was exultant as she parted with her treasure chest of synthesis. . . . I was dumbfounded. The horoscope looked like numbered alphabet soup patterns. I couldn't study it, take it apart; I could only view it like an aberrant impressionistic painting. She hadn't drawn her horoscope; she had Jackson-Pollacked it!

Finally she finished. ". . .and the Part of Love of God, which is the Part of Faith plus the Part of Expectancy minus the sum of the Part of Imprisonment, Sorrow, and Captivity and the Part of Slavery and Bondage."

Remarkable. Her Taurus structuring instinct had run wild. Her Leo Ascendant had constructed its own mighty pedestal. Her theatricality was so convincing. I had no recourse except to co-operate: "Alright, Miss Fortunata, what's bothering you about your Parts?" (That didn't sound quite right, but she understood perfectly.)

"Well, I've watched all of this quite carefully over the past four years, Mr. Mercury." She began her presentation: "I'm fortunate to have an inheritance, from my father— you can see that from the Part of the Father at 11 Sagittarius sextile the Part of Friends at 11 Aquarius. . . . I invented that symbol: a smile . . . really a Moon . . . holding friendship within it . . . square the part of Expectancy at

11 Virgo (the HO in a square represents self-contained Hope) . . . and the Part of Inheritance and Possessions at 6 Cancer in the XIIth (and this Part rules the VIIIth, you know) . . . . so, with my inheritance I have lots of time to do astrology, and I've checked and rechecked every day . . . especially last Thursday, when the transiting Part of Fortune . . . interesting that this Part is my namesake, wouldn't you say? . . . when it came to a Vigintile aspect . . . . that's 18 degrees: very, very subtly good, don't you agree? . . . with my Part of Astrology at 18 Aquarius . . . . I just knew I had to talk with you, to get your support of my system. . . . I am so thrill—"

I had to interrupt "Please, Miss Fortune . . . Miss Fortunata. I appreciate your enthusiasm. I see your point. I don't know about last Thursday, but please let me ask a few questions.   What is this 'PU' at your Midheaven?"

"Oh, I'm so glad you asked. THAT's my Part of Understanding. It's square my Part of Surgery in the VIth in 28 Capricorn; it is really a good . . . ."

"Part of Surgery . . . you mean KN? What's KN mean?"

"Knife."

"Oh."

"Yes . . . to make it easier, let's just abbreviate: KN is squared by PU in my MH. It means that my understanding of my life is incisive, cuts like a knife, forcefully to lead my sense of duty and service through astrology."

"Oh. And this Part at 11 Leo, the four lines with a dome?"

"Oh, Mr. Mercury, you're soooo observant. You

really get to the heart of the matter quickly. I knew *you* would. I just knew it. That's the Part of Imprisonment . . . . those are bars covered by a rainbow."

"Oh."

"But you *do* see that it is opposing my Part of Friends . . . remember the Moon-smile, but trine my Part of Father in the Vth . . . just past a Vigintile aspect with the Love of God Part."

"That would mean that you have trouble communicating your theories to your friends; that you feel self-imprisonment; that your father warned you about this, and you know that your love of God will lead you to acceptance and illumination eventually?"

"Mr. Mercury, you're a genius! I'm overwhelmed. You *do* understand."

"Yes I do, Miss Fortunata, partly. But I'm very curious about the motive behind all this work . . . where did you get the idea of dispensing with the planets?"

And, when I asked this question, her mood changed sharply . . . . the pride seemed lost. Maybe my *own* Part of Gambling—whatever that is—was taking over. I had a hunch. I had identified with her, and I now had a hunch about what was tearing her personality apart. She looked away for the first time. She seemed caught in sadness of memory, fear of future.

She began her explanation carefully, tentatively, with clear embarrassment: "I *have* dispensed with the planets, Mr. Mercury. But I *do* remember them. . . especially the Sun. My birth date . . . and my study of astrology ruined my life temporarily . . . . I had to find a way to get away from the meanings of my birth date, my Sun position. And I've met many who feel the same way."

As soon as she said this, I knew my hunch had been right. She was born on May 17. Her Sun was in the 27th degree of Taurus . . . . *the position of the fixed Star Algol.* This was difficult, maybe dangerous. I remember cautioning myself; I didn't want to lose my head at this point.

After a slight. pause, she continued: "The only concession I've made to my birthright is in the naming of my pet snake . . . ."

Startled, I interrupted: "You've named your pet snake Algol . . . or Medusa?"

"Oh, Mr. Mercury, you do understand . . . even this, you understand," she said almost worshipfully, "my snake is named Medusa, whose head of snakehair is formed by Algol in the constellation Persei."

"But Miss Fortunata, how is it that this observation was so traumatic for you?"

"When I began to study astrology, I decided to begin with astronomy, to really get a grounding in the heavens, and the literature and legends about Algol overwhelmed me. I'd look at my Sun and only see Algol; it began to pursue me . . . . so I resolved to play into its hands partially and I bought my pet snake . . . as a reminder of my destiny. Then I worked night and day to synthesize all the bodies in my horoscope, to found a new branch of Astrology . . . something like Astro-Partology, 'ASP' . . . to get away from planetary units and structure, and identity of inter-relationships, a system of synthesis that would truly inter-relate all nuances of life experience."

Really, I had to hand it to her. She was so convincing. She believed in her research. I was not to gain anything by disagreeing. I had to play along. Maybe there was a way to return her fearless to her Sun.

"Now look, Miss Fortunata, I too have studied astronomy and I can identify with your fears about Algol. Indeed, they are over-rated by many students, but, then again, the *fears* can be very, very real. Let me share with you some private research I have made into this."

And here I began a tale . . . perhaps not complete fabrication . . . but a tale with enough historical references to be believed and enough emotional significance to be therapeutic. I had to cooperate with her fantasy in order to reach her.

"Nicolas Oresme, who died in 1382, was a French bishop. He was an arch-critic of the occult, but did not negate astrology. He attacked certain astrologers, but left the heavenly mysteria alone. I came across a Latin text of his while doing research in the Sorbonne Library last summer, during a vacation trip to Paris. It was fascinating, because it dealt with Oresme's private diary of *his* research. He made astrological postulations of his own for the day when his own skill might mature or wisdom be revealed, when he might share them with the world. About the so-called fixed Stars, his notes were *epic!*"

As I created data on the spot, Miss Fortunata's eyes hardly blinked. New knowledge was going into her like water into a dry plant. I spun legend after legend, all in connection with the Star supposedly postulated by Oresme, *Stella Ego Redemptionis*, the Star of Self-redemption.

This Star, Oresme maintained, crowned a Constellation newly formed by the Precession movement at the time of the baptism of Christ. This Star, which he abbreviated to 'Redemptor,' was significant for 'Self-redemption after hardship.' This Constellation again was clearly noted by ancient scribes at the time of the Crucifixion . . . . *also* a kind of Baptism and Redemption."

By this time, Miss Fortunata was agape with wonder. And I was really enjoying it. My Moon in Leo was really performing! I took her through a truly remarkable string of references to Self-Redemption in history, bringing in Charlemagne, Martin Luther, Tolstoi, Rudolf Hess, even Malcolm X.

"And, of course, many people, famous and not famous, have the chance to redeem themselves. This Star, like any other, falls in *every* horoscope, at an important point or at an unimportant point. It all depends on the need of the identify in life. . . . "

"But why don't the books today have this Star in them?" she said as if interrupted from a dream.

I had to search hard for an explanation to that one, but it came quickly: "After Christ's Resurrection, the Star was eclipsed . . . . occultists said the light of the Redeemer Himself took the place of the light of the Star. But, Miss Fortunata, the most important thing is that the Star is still there; it sends out no light, but its position is a point . . . . a *part*, if you will, of Symbolic Remembrance of Messianic Grandeur, SRMG."

We both paused. It was magic. I was believing myself easily. In fact, everything I said seemed so right. I made mental notes to fantasize more often. Truths seemed to appear even in cartoon fashion, from some unconscious store-house.

"Miss Fortunata," I resumed, "this Star is in *your* horoscope as well, at a very critical and *positive* point. *It is conjunct your Ascendant!*"

She was shocked into a gasp, an intaking of air . . . an inspiration, literally, that took in all I said. She filled up with a new strength.

"Really? Are you sure?"

"Yes, I'm sure. I usually ignore it; *never* have I talked about it to clients. But it's there. Yours is the first case where the need is so great to know where the Star is. Algol has led you to find it. Awareness brings recognition. You've *earned* it."

At this moment, she rose to her feet, her eyes filled with tears. I rose too, and we both smiled. She needed no more explanation. I handed back her horoscope. She folded it without looking at it and put it into her shopping bag. "A reminder," was all she said.

We walked to the door, and I said to her: "Doing Parts, studying synthesis is all well and good, Miss Fortunata, but overdoing it takes away the integrity, the value of the individual components. What happens when you stir or blend pancake batter too much? (She smiled quickly.) The pancakes lose their 'personality,' right?"

"Right. And thank you so much, Mr. Mercury. You're an absolute genius. You've given me new faith. I'll get back on the track, I promise."

"And wash Algol out of your hair?"

"Yes," she laughed.

"And get rid of your snake?"

"Absolutely—and thank you, Mr. Mercury; I'll call you again soon, if I may."

"Of course, and thank *you*. I've really enjoyed it. We were partners there for a while!"

The last phrase lingered with me after she left. We *were* partners, regardless of the pun I had tried to make. And that's what astrology's all about: partnership and dialogue. But I had made up practically everything I had said. I could never allow that in astrology. But her horoscope . . . her 'Partoscope' had led us far afield to begin with. I wasn't giving her astrological advice by any means . . . . we both were on detours and ended up back on the main road. But that Star, what a story!  Might it be on everyone's Ascendant?

"Can Astrology play detective?"

## Chapter Three

### THE CASE OF THE THESPIAN MARS

The subways certainly announce springtime! As soon as the Vernal Equinox takes place, some engineer somewhere in Brooklyn—maybe his name is Vernon—turns on a steam valve to humidify the underground. Pluto should rule steam and discomfort. It was already mid-summer below and coolingly the end of March above.

"Guh Moanin,' Mr. Merc'ry," the newsman said.

Wonder how long Sam's been here. Fifty-ninth and Lexington, some home! Sam's *always* here, always cheerful, but after all these years of "Good Mornings and Good Nights," Sam won't part with his birth information . . . and I can't figure him out. Newspapers and magazines are ruled by Mercury and the third house, but he doesn't look Gemini-ish or Virgo-ish. Wonder how *his* life fluctuates . . . probably through the weather, good customers and bad . . . quite a puzzle . . . why's he so private about himself?

"Good Morning, Sam, it's a lot cooler up *here* than down *there*."

"Dat's for shoah, Mr. Merc'ry, ya'll nevah fahnd me in dem subways, no suh!"

Well, how does Sam get home? Where does he live? Maybe he lives in his paper-stall? "Thanks, Sam;" I took my *New York Times* and went into the arcade, down the hallway, just made it into the elevator. Another people-crush: ten or eleven horoscopes jammed into a Muzak moment together, each one pretending the others don't exist. I got off at 'five' and headed down the hall to my office. Love that door: Cally's idea of dark blue was really comforting . . . the white lettering too. She's a great gal . . . and that name 'Fardina Callisto' . . . and jovial to boot . . . "Good Morning, *Cally*!"

"Good Morning, Merk! Mrs. Haley just called to cancel her 9 o'clock, so calm down. Would you like me to bring in some coffee?"

"Oh. Fine *Cally*. Thanks . . . did Mrs. Haley say why she cancelled?"

"Nope, no *comet* at all."

Cally's puns always got us off to a good start. She's great and really learning astrology.

My office was comfortably cool, on the western side of the building. This would be a good morning: the charts were ready for 11 and that IRC group. I'll really be able to help them with those personnel selections.

"Thank you, Cally . . . that was fast. Here, sit down with me; you're not busy right now, are you?"

She put the coffee on the table and sat with me on

the brown sofa. "No, I'm all caught up, but please let me ask you about a problem I'm having with Von Schadow's system for Primary Directions. I'm really in the dark . . . ."

Dear Cally went on with her problem. I skipped the headlines . . . Vietnam, Vietnam . . . endless . . . and went to the drama page. Stella and I were to go to that opening last night, but her bronchitis was so bad, we were afraid we'd ruin everything with her coughing. The Saturn-Mars conjunction on her Mercury in Gemini really has laid her low. Mr. Wentworth certainly was disappointed, but I'm sure they found other guests for the tickets . . . I began to read Alice Antagona's review: *"Cathedral in the Park* . . . a real hit . . .realism and humor bring Paula Catherine's talent to national prominence . . . " A real hit, and we missed it! This Paula Catherine must be some actress . . . on the cover of *TIME* last week, even before the opening . . . .

"Please, Merk, help me with this," Cally interrupted. "Why do we have to interpolate for latitude when the measurements are so tedious and the result seems so little?"

What a question! I'd given up all these endless measurements long ago. We astrologers weren't writing books for Kings anymore. And what one could measure down to infinitesimal points was usually observable also in other, easier measurements. But the exercise is good for any student . . . "Cally, after you subtract the Right Ascension and then multiply the Latitude fraction-over-sixty by the difference, you get a significant number . . . then you observe the rule about increasing or decreasing from one Latitude to the next . . . and you're near the arc of . . . "

The telephone saved me! I picked up the extension: "Michael Mercury."

"Mr. Mercury, this is John Backer." The voice was deep, slow; sounded exhausted.

"Yes, Mr. Backer?" I wrote his name on the pad.

"Mr. Mercury, we—I need your help. My wife died last night, and . . . "

"Oh, I'm sorry, Mr. Backer."

" . . . and maybe you can help. My wife is the actress Paula Catherine."

I was dumbfounded. Shocked. Mr. Backer obviously sensed it. We both were silent for a moment of recognition.

"But Mr. Backer, I've just been reading the review of her play-opening last night . . . how can this be . . . what's happened?" I was almost speechless.

"You've been reading a very early edition. The later editions carry the story on page one." He was almost muffled with fatigue. "Paula was found dead in her dressing room early this morning, about 3:30. She died, the police think, just before 2 AM. She never appeared at the Waldorf Reception, and finally I went back to the theatre to see if anything was wrong, and the night-watchman and I found her."

"Oh my!" I was still stunned.

"These openings are such nerve-wracking affairs. Paula insists on being alone in preparation and, after the performances, with all the visitors back-stage, I always stay away. I was with the cast and producers at the Waldorf waiting for her . . . for her entrance . . . and then made the trip back to the theatre when she didn't show up." Mr. Backer shifted subjects and tone abruptly. "I'm calling for your help, Mr. Mercury. You've got quite a reputation. May I come see you right away?"

"Yes, yes, of course. How soon can you be here?"

"In half an hour."

"Fine."

"But you'll need Paula's birth information, won't you?"

"Yes, yes . . . you *do* have it?"

"Yes. I checked her papers this morning and I have her birth certificate," I cradled the phone between my neck and shoulder, held the pad steady with my left hand and took down the information: "and it says clearly that she was born at 7:04 PM, in the evening, May 23, 1942 in London . . . and there's an interesting note that the birth occurred *in* Saint Paul's Cathedral . . . I don't know if that's significant, but it is noted on the birth certificate."

"*In* Saint Paul's Cathedral?" I questioned.

"Yes."

"Fine. Alright. I have the information. I'll be ready for you at 9:45."

"Thank you, Mr. Mercury, good-bye."

I hung up the phone still stunned. The paper was still on my lap, open to the review. There was Paula Catherine's photo: strong, large head, deep eyes . . . the features of an actress . . . to project emotion to the highest balcony . . . the dark strong hair . . . probably a Scorpio Ascendant. . . . early Gemini birth . . . I went to my desk to work on the chart. Cally knew there was a crisis. I explained quickly. She shared the shock . . . our day had begun.

I worked out the birth horoscope and noted the transit positions for early that morning. Cally went out and found a late-edition morning paper. The details were on on page one: found dead by her husband and the night-watchman at 3:30 AM, cause of death not yet determined, no evidence of struggle . . . etc.

Staring at the horoscope, I saw the actress: there was that Scorpio Ascendant as I had expected . . . and the VIIIth House Gemini Sun . . . double Summer Time in England in 1942 had altered the Sun position somewhat, working with a corrected Standard Time of 5:04 PM. That Sun was conjoined with Saturn and Uranus! trined by Neptune: unique ambition, Self-searching creativity, fantasy, inspiration, unusual friends . . . sextile to Pluto, confirmation of the Ascendant, public projection . . . in Leo . . . drama . . . Leo Mid-Heaven; square to the Sun group from the Moon . . . in Virgo in the Xth: family upheaval at birth? The drive to make something of herself, highly critical professional projection of her personality . . . alluring . . . near the North node . . . Jupiter-Mercury conjunction in Gemini . . . wow! That's communication, squaring Neptune . . . uh-huh . . . and Mars square Venus . . . foreign husband . . . tension . . . high-level sense of service in the arts. . . . Backer was an American, no doubt . . . and Pluto was square the Ascendant, Venus trine the mid-Heaven.  Here *was* a powerful actress for sure!

The transits were frightening: Saturn and Mars . . . Stella's coughing . . . were exactly . . . EXACTLY in conjunction then, on the Saturn-Sun-Uranus group! Uranus was squaring the birth Mars from the XIIth! Moon nearing

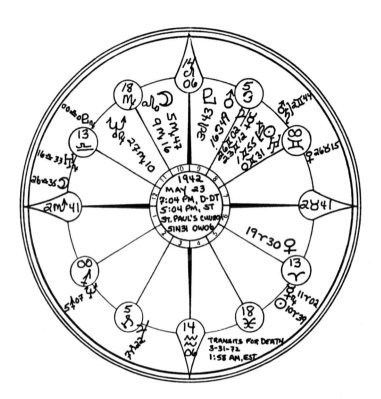

Ascendant. Sun and Mercury in conjunction in the Vth . . .
Neptune opposing the problems in the VIIIth.

I put the horoscope down. Cleared my desk of papers.
The picture was clear . . . this actress was at an incredibly
powerful turning point of her life. Saturn's return . . . the
Pluto transit trining the group . . . Saturn-Mars, Neptune . . .
murder? . . . poison? . . . VIIIth House . . . the birth Mars-
Venus . . . that would need study . . . art, yes, sex tension
. . . all these things are vital to an actress, but they invite
trouble as well.

Cally buzzed. Mr. Backer had arrived.

As he came into my office, my mind was so taken up
with his wife's measurements that I worked to concentrate
on him. He was strong looking, affluent, well-dressed . . .
his sadness and shock drained the color from his face. His
graying, Cary Grant style hair was disheveled by worry.

"Mr. Mercury, thank you for seeing me so quickly.
May I sit down please?"

Mr. Backer crumpled into the chair before my desk.

"Mr. Backer, how can I help you? I've done the horoscope. It's crucially dramatic for this time. But often these
symbols correspond to great growth and success as well as
or at the same time as, great difficulty. Death is something
we don't look for, can't reasonably see. Let me ask, was it
a natural death? Have you gotten the police lab reports?

"Yes . . . they phoned me just as I was leaving to
come here. They say she had been dead about one and a
half hours, probably just before two, as I told you. Death
came from a blow to the forehead."

"Did she fall?"

"She could have, but the body was at such an angle as hardly to make that possible. Her dressing-room was heavily carpeted, and we found her on her back."

"Do the police think someone else could have. . . . "

"Yes, they do. They think someone came into her dressing room as she was about to leave and join the reception . . . after all the back-stage visitors and fans had left . . . after she had changed clothes . . . and struck her powerfully on her head."

We stopped talking. A blow to the head . . . there's that Mars-Venus potential . . . Venus in Aries . . . in such a dramatic personality . . . a tease . . . .

"Mr. Backer, is there any cause to suspect that she could have in any way provoked such an attack?"

"That's a hard question, Mr. Mercury. Paula . . . and you know, on the way over here I realized where she had got her stage name: from St. Paul's Cathedral, where she had been born! She had never mentioned that to a soul, not even to me . . . . "

"Yes, I would have expected that. Eighth House Suns are so secretive, and the Scorpio Ascendant . . . and other measurements. I think there must have been an air raid while Paula's mother was trying to get to a hospital—it was during the War—and she took refuge in the Cathedral . . . that would explain the upheaval at the time of birth . . . that I see in the chart . . . it probably meant a lot to her as she studied her own life . . . that unique beginning."

"I see . . . anyway . . . about provacation . . . Paula had a way about her, a teasing way. She was so strong and forceful . . . but her nerves were like sparks . . . she had migraine headaches . . . everything she touched gained a tremendous force. She would instantly get to the deepest part of her roles. But, at the same time, she 'played' with people's personalities. She spotted weaknesses and little flaws, and dramatized them in her unique way. These perceptions are what made her the superb actress she was, but they had a way of roping people into her control, against their will . . . no . . .   better: without their knowing it."

"Her Venus in Aries would certainly correspond to such behavior."

"Mr. Mercury, I really don't understand all your planet-talk, but I do know astrology can do amazing things. Your reputation . . . and the way theatre people believe in occult things . . . well, on impulse, I called you this morning. I haven't slept . . . I need some help . . . can you do something . . . can astrology . . . uh . . . 'play detective'?"

'Play detective.' The words were a challenge and a responsibility. Every astrologer's imagination plays detective with news stories, with people on subways. It's good practice. But to be really helpful here? . . . It could be done . . . It's reasonable to assume that *everything* is in the horoscope . . . we just have to be good enough to see it.

"Mr. Backer, I think we *can* . . . *astrology* can. It's difficult, but I'm willing to try . . . right away . . . but," my mind started racing ahead: I didn't want to get involved with the police investigation and all the explanations that would be necessary . . . back-stage areas are so protected, outsiders can't really get in there . . . surely everyone had left . . . Paula had changed her clothes . . . the watchman hadn't seen anything unusual . . . someone knew his way around the theatre . . . Paula would have admitted him or her without fear or suspicion . . . an inside job, as they say . . . but I'll need something from you."

"What? Anything."

"Please go into my secretary's office and use the phone there. Somehow, get a list of all the theatre's personnel . . . all concerned with the show and the management . . . anyone Paula would have seen or known during the rehearsals and preparations in the theatre. That means office people, stage-hands, ticket-sellers, advertising people, assistants in all departments, etc. Maybe we can get the list together quickly from employment records in the producer's office, and someone can send them over right away by messenger. Just a list of names and duties performed . . . *and their birthdates*, if possible."

"But I don't see why, Mr. Mercury. The police surely have this same information and are checking them all out."

"Yes. I'm sure too, but we're using astrology . . . we'll do our checking from right here in this room! Please, Mr. Backer . . . I'm going to try to help, and *you've* got to help me." I escorted him to the door, and Cally rose to meet us.

"Cally, please help Mr. Backer with some phone calls; call IRC and change the appointment to late afternoon . . . they'll understand . . . or tomorrow . . . shift all afternoon appointments a couple hours later . . . no explanations to anyone . . . and bring in some more coffee for me, OK?"

I didn't even wait for Cally's inevitable stream of questions. I returned to my office, closed the door, and began reviewing all the horary and dynamic house-reading systems I'd ever studied. The birth chart would surely show the entire picture, if I could just see it clearly. This was tricky business . . . but I had to measure deductions so carefully and build some sort of conclusion . . . the list would be corroboration when it came . . . I had to keep myself out of it and try to let the chart speak for itself . . . as detailed as possible.

I ordered my room so there would be no distractions. Only the horoscope and a pad were on my desk. Mars would undoubtedly be the key here . . . it was crucial in the birth horoscope . . . it came out in our conversation . . . her head had been struck . . . in a theatre . . . the Venus square. I started to make notes on my pad:

"Transit Mars has 'hit' the Sun, the Life Energy, in the House of Death. Saturn has returned . . . ambition fulfilled . . . or frustrated. With transiting Mars in the VIIIth, second of the VIIth: a hit, a blow for ambition, jealousy, from another about another's own values? Sudden attack. Uranus there natally. Against another's eccentricity, unusual success. Success invites jealousy.

"The Uranus role echoed by transit square to natal Mars from the XIIth: the jealous clash from an institution, from a hidden enemy, within the organization?

"Neptune opposing the Mars-Saturn transit: theatrical camouflage; in the IInd, again Paula's resources, marketable talent opposing that of another.

"Sun and Mercury-retrograde transit, in Mars' Sign: Transiting Mercury, ruler of Gemini, the

> Sun Sign, retrograde in the Vth . . . coming back-
> stage in a theatre . . . *worker* in the theatre, com-
> ing back from the VIth . . . and the Vth would
> be the eleventh of the VIIth . . . the hopes and
> wishes of the 'other.' "

So far so good. I could hear Mr. Backer faintly in the
other room. Cally had obviously forgotten the coffee.
Time was flying, but I was on the track: someone inside
the theatre, probably hoping for a career like Paula's, a co-
worker, jealous of her enormous success, maybe infuriated
. . . poisoned by her teasing ways . . . couldn't take it any
more, came back-stage . . . maybe gained entrance through
false compliments and flattery . . . then maybe, when teased
again, exploded . . . struck Paula on the head. With what?

With what? That was a key. Venus was attacked in
every way symbolically. I made some more notes:

> "Venus rules the VIIth and the XIIth: further
> corroboration of the other's jealousy, animosity
> . . . art-frustration . . . in the VIth, worker. Venus
> in transit was in the VIIth trine Paula's Neptune:
> the murderer's work and art roles were part of
> Paula's magic structure, but the other's hopes
> couldn't stand the frustration. And the fixed
> star Algol was conjoined by this transiting Ve-
> nus." I recalled a case I had had about Algol
> the year before. The head blow . . . Medusa.

It was clear: Venus and Mars were the keys in every
way. Mars was the murderer and Venus the means . . . Mars
was the reaction and Venus the provocation, the entice-
ment. I thought further, losing all track of time: if this

*were* so, the murderer could possibly be a Cancer . . . that's where Paula's birth Mars was. The natal square with Venus; and the Sun problem area was very near the semi-square mid-point of the major square. Definitely, here was the deadly focus.

What would Mr. Cancer use?   I was sure it had to be a man: Mars is male, the IXth House where Mars was positioned is male, the Gemini attack focus is male, Aries is male. Cancer's femininity was over-ruled.   Venus: the man would've used a hand implement, the Gemini focus . . . could it have been a piece of Paula's jewelry . . . not heavy enough . . . a statuette she might have had as a good-luck piece . . . It would have been broken with the blow, probably, and the police would have mentioned it . . . Mr. Backer would have mentioned it.

I went to my bookcase and took out Lorna Schornstein's *Glossary of Rulerships*. I sped through the pages and pages of Venus rulerships . . . waiting to discover a "theatrical weapon."   I had it! It jumped off the page at me: *a flashlight!* All my feelings and deductions fell into place . . . It had to be true. A jealous co-worker killed Paula with a flashlight! *Ushers* use flash-lights: ushers are ruled by Mercury . . . coming back-stage . . . retrograde into the Vth, into the theatre from the VIth . . . workers. It fit. Everything checked. I went around and around and around the wheel and again I WAS SURE.

I looked at my watch: an hour and fifteen minutes had passed. I was exhausted. I buzzed Cally: "Cally, please bring Mr. Backer in . . . and some coffee please."

"Merk, Mr. Backer's downstairs waiting for the messenger. They're sending the personnel files over immediately. I'll be right in."

We drank the coffee in silence. It was totally clear to me: an usher murdered Paula, with his flashlight, in a sudden jealous rage, teased by the star on her big night, when his pleas . . . perhaps . . . when his pleas for her help with *his* career evoked Paula's provocative sarcasm.

Cally knew not to interrupt my thoughts. There was more . . . that transiting Saturn with Mars . . . maybe a description of the usher: slender, introverted, dark eyes, a loner . . . fired dreams way ahead of his abilities . . . maybe an Aries Ascendant supplying the potential of explosion, the Ego thrust . . . maybe that was going too far.

Mr. Backer burst into the outer office and came running into the room: "Here are the lists, here they are. What do we do now?"

I took the lists out of the envelopes. They were ar ranged by department: 'Cast, Stage Crew. Box Office, Producer's Office, Publicity, Special Services.' That was the one . . . 'Special Services.' The list had 15 make-up assistants, four policemen, three chauffeurs . . . then: 20 ushers. I put the other papers aside: 20 ushers . . . 12 women and 8 men.

I stood up and took this list of names to my desk. Cally and Mr. Backer stood by silently. I must have looked like Merlin—or better, Perry Mason. I was transported into my symbolic deductions. Which of these 8 men was I 'divining' . . . and *that* was the right word for it!

'December 11, July 9, July 2, June 19, October 26, January 9, April 13, April 29.' Two Cancers: July 9 and July 2.

"Please sit down," I said to Cally and Mr. Backer, "you're making me nervous. I'm on to something, I think; just give me a few more minutes."

The two names were O. Shenton and W. Brinstor. Was it possible to decide . . . then it hit me: the Mars position was 16 Cancer . . . the Sun would have been in the 16th degree of Cancer on July 8th or 9th! O. Shenton was born July 9!   My Lord! could it be possible . . . was I right? . . . was everything really in every horoscope . . . only for us to be lucky or skilled enough . . . inspired enough to find it? Then, the final wave of intuition hit me . . . I picked up Schornstein's book again and searched under 'letters:' 'O' was the letter of Mars . . . ! 'Sh' was a special aspirated sound . . . AND IT WAS GOVERNED BY CANCER!

I must have appeared about to faint. Cally and Mr. Backer interrupted: "Are you all right? What's wrong?"

I recovered my composure and began: "Mr. Backer, I can hardly believe it, but I think astrology has given us a tremendously significant lead. It checks out so thoroughly, it's hard to think that it's not *the* answer."

Backer's eyes, even though puffed with strain and fatigue, widened as he sat forward on the edge of his chair. Cally too was tense, mystified.

"From my work, I think an associate of Paula's murdered her in a sudden jealous rage, perhaps provoked by Paula's teasing way. It would have been someone she knew, for him to get into her dressing room, not to have invited a struggle."

"Mr. Mercury, you say 'him;' you think it was a man . . . and not . . . a . . . a . . . an understudy or something like that?" Becker asked.

"No, I feel confident that it was a man. And, Mr. Backer . . . often in astrology certain things happen in horoscopes that seem almost magical. It's a dangerous thing, calling for much discipline and experience on the part of the astrologer. Well, certain inter-relationships, which I've checked and re-checked many times, seem to indicate that Paula may have been murdered by a male usher."

"An USHER?" they both asked, practically shouting.

"Yes. I think an usher waited around till after everyone had gone, came back-stage to see Paula, flattered her, got into her dressing room, and pleaded for her assistance in advancing his career. I think she provoked him, and he exploded . . . and, I think" —my words were hesitant— "that he struck her violently on the forehead with a flashlight."

"A flashlight!!!!? Really, Mr. Mercury, I don't . . . I can't . . . "

"Yes, I know it sounds preposterous to read such details from a horoscope. But I've done the best I can. From the personnel lists, I've checked all the ushers' names . . . and I think the murderer might be this one here—O. Shenton, judging from his birthday and the prominent letters of his name."

"But this is impossible. We can't accuse an innocent man . . . another person, just like that, " and he snapped his fingers.

"Of course we can't," I replied, "But, look, take this tip to the police; don't tell them where it came from; just beg them to investigate it immediately. Nothing will be lost. They'll undoubtedly investigate all personnel eventually, the ushers last . . . or even first . . . but the point is the sooner the better for this man. Let's find out. I can't intercede because I'd have to explain all about astrology and break down their bias first. *You* can go there directly and tell the detectives your information . . . and get some action right away. Please . . . do this . . . it's terribly important . . . I've done all I possibly can."

I had hardly finished my sentence, and Backer flew out of the office. No good-bye's, no thank-you's. We did hear "I'll call you" from the outer hall, but he just ran out of the office. It was noon-time. I was exhausted. Cally brought up some sandwiches, and we ate quickly, trying to calm down for the long afternoon of postponed appointments.

I had a short nap, awoke refreshed, and started in. At 4:45, Cally interrupted me with the call from Mr. Backer:

"Mercury, the police were cooperative and they've got this man Shenton in the questioning room now. He's an acting student, lives alone, very tall, swarthy, with quite a jagged, sharp look to him. He looks scared. He looks like our man! I didn't thank you when I left, but you must know my gratitude . . . I'll call you again when the interrogation is finished."

Backer's description of Shenton turned my adrenalin on again. We were close . . . just maybe this *was* the man.

My meeting with IRC lasted until 9:00 PM. It was quite successful. And I left the office truly drained. Stella would never believe this day. Backer hadn't called me back.

"Gud Ev'nin,' Mr. Merc'ry," Sam said, "Workin' late tuhnaht?"

"Yes, Sam, it was a big day."

"It shooh was, Mr. Merc'ry: dey already caught dat man who done dat attress in! Heah's da naht edition of da Telly."

I hardly heard Sam's words . . . I grabbed the paper, and my eyes swept across the front page: headlines . . . "USHER CONFESSES ACTRESS MURDER—Thousands to attend St. Patrick Burial Thursday."

"Guhnaht, Mr. Merc'ry."

I couldn't go into the subway. I had to walk. It was too dark to read in the street . . . I just had to walk and relive the tension . . . the goose-bumps that covered me. I went west across Park, then across Madison, cut down to 53rd, crossed to Fifth Avenue, and walked down to Rockefeller Center. I'd get a cab there. No subway tonight.

I hailed a cab just one block from St. Patrick's. As I ducked down to get into the cab, my eyes caught the outline of the Cathedral. It would be Paula's last appearance. Quite a dramatic exit. I remembered St. Paul's. Quite a dramatic place to be born.

*. . .Astrology solved a critical problem.*

Chapter Four

## THE CASE OF THE PLUNDERED PLUTONIUM

Raining cats and dogs! Yet, several hundred astrology buffs were hanging up raincoats and umbrellas in the foyer of Rice College Auditorium. I had enjoyed my week in Houston, conferring with NASA about timing Moonshots. The lecture invitation at Rice had coincided neatly with my meetings.

The lecture subject was to be Horary Astrology . . . quite difficult. Horary Astrology is such a personal form of the astrological art. It's hard to give "rules" and procedures to two hundred students at one time. But, then again, it was gratifying to know that 200 or so really were trying hard to learn. Astrology was really enjoying a revival across the nation.

I was ushered back to my dressing room. From the doorway, I could see the stage, and I noted that the rostrum

and slide-screen were in good position. There wasn't much
more to prepare. I did feel a bit uneasy though, because
tonight, I was going to lecture with material I'd never used,
never shared before. It would surprise the audience for
sure, and I wanted to be at my best.

I gave Mrs. Archer, the enthusiastic President of the
Houston-Galveston Astrology Association, the chart-slides
I would need, and she promised they would be projected
upon the screen as soon as I asked for them.

We were already five minutes late because of the rain,
parking and coat problems. I was anxious to begin.

Mrs. Archer walked onto the stage and received a
warm reception. She began the introduction.

"Ladies and gentlemen . . . and it *is* goood to have
the gentlemen here with us tonaaht . . ."

I always wondered why not enough men were involved
with Astrology. I guess they simply don't have enough
time to take on the study. But it seemed that things were
improving all over the country . . .

"You know that ouwah guest tonaaht is the famous
Michael Mercury from New Yawk."

More applause. That's nice.

"Tonaaht will be a special one, Mr. Mercury has as-
sured me: he's speakin' about an experience that has been
top secret for many years."

The ladies oohed and ahhed.   Well, they should. This
ought to be one hell of a lecture!

"So, without takin' any more taahm than necessary, I
want to proudly introduce MISTER MICHAEL MER-CU-
RY."

There was heavy applause as I walked out to the center of the stage and shook hands with Mrs. Archer. I remembered how pleased I was that she had taken off her hat . . . or not put one on . . . for her appearance. So often women do that at these lectures . . . I don't understand it . . . and it's fascinating how these little things pop into your head during important moments. It's as if a stage spotlight closes in your perceptions before expanding them, like the pupil of your eye adjusting to brighter light. I accepted the applause and made myself as comfortable as I could at the lecturn.

"Good evening, gentlemen and ladies," I began . . . and they laughed nicely . . . good audience. "This is an important night for me. Not only because of your kind invitation, but because I want to share with you quite an exciting story, one that indeed has been secret—top, top secret—for *twenty-eight* years!"

Again an alert and hushed response. This was going to be a fine night.

"I'm going to get right to the heart of the story. It's so fascinating, and I want us to have time for many questions at the end of my talk." I paused for the sake of drama. "I can now tell you, since the secrecy ban on this information has just been lifted, that astrology . . . that an *astrologer*! was crucially involved in the last days of the Manhattan Project in the Spring of 1945 . . . the Manhattan Project, of course, was the code name for the Atomic Bomb!"

Everyone, except for me, shifted position in the auditorium. This was high drama. Everyone had something to say out of nervousness or surprise, There was a buzzing throughout the large hall. I let it subside of its own accord.

"Yes, as much maligned as astrology is by people who have no idea about it . . . it just *is not* what we read too easily and often in popular magazines and newspapers . . . astrology was indeed the vital link, during a moment of crisis, that helped the War, that made the Atomic Bomb possible. Now, please don't misunderstand: we are not arguing the ethics of the bomb or its use, and I don't mean to imply that astrology had anything to do with the *discovery* of the Bomb and its workings. As I tell you the story, you'll see that astrology *solved a critical problem*.

"Let me start at the beginning: the Manhattan Project was the biggest military and political secret of all time. Not even Vice President Truman knew about it until he took office upon Roosevelt's death in April 1945. The astrologer Bruno Einblick was the man who also shared the secret one month later in May. Einblick was a German who had been in America since 1909. He had become a citizen in 1920. You all know his writings under the pen-name Seraphim Gabriel." Another flurry of whispered comments brought the sea of faces to life. Einblick's books were in every astrologer's library.

"Einblick chose that pseudonym because he felt no one would believe his real name as the real name of an astrologer. 'Einblick' means 'insight' in German. So to be more credible, he chose the name under which we have enjoyed him so and learned so much. In 1945, he was 63 years old, a grand master of astrology.

"Einblick lived in Washington and had a prestigious clientele among diplomats from many nations. He could speak English, French, Hungarian, Italian, Spanish, and, of course, German. His ethical silence was exemplary. The man was trusted by all.

"Upon his death in 1965, his private papers were turned over by the Bank of North America to my teacher, Edward Clyptic, with whom I am still in close contact . . . and *he* has shared the details with me. The recent publication of the Stromberg Papers, the death of President Truman, and the expiration of the secrecy statute put on the Project allow us now to share Einblick's part in the Project.

"Einblick was awakened in the very early morning on Wednesday, May 30, 1945. His diary records the time of the call as 4:02 AM. A highly authoritative, secretive voice requested Einblick's immediate appearance in an old Civil Service office building on Massachusetts Avenue in Washington. The caller made it very clear how important and confidential this was. He told Einblick that in 20 minutes, a private car would be waiting for him at his door and that the driver would identify himself with a phrase that would have immediate significance for Einblick.

"We can imagine this great man, rising quickly, dressing, gathering his tables, his mind racing in preparation for the calculations and deductions he knew he would have to make.   Einblick records that he left his apartment at 4:35. A car was parked in front of the apartment house entrance. The driver rolled down his window and said 'Herr Einblick, die Sterne beeinflussen; sie erzwingen nicht, doch alle

Sachen haben ihre eigene Zeit.' This immediately identified
the driver and gained Einblick's trust. The man had said:
'The stars incline, they do not compel, yet all things have
their own time.' Einblick had written those words himself
in a philosophy doctoral thesis at Harvard in 1923. He got
into the car, and they sped off.

"Traffic was non-existent at that early hour, and in
10 minutes the car pulled up at the dark office building.
They entered, and Einblick noted that they went through
several doors, lit only by tiny red bulbs above the door
frames, then into a very small elevator that stopped four
floors up. There were three men in the hallway there; they
didn't move or speak, and Einblick was ushered into a
room at the end of the corridor.

"Einblick described the room in great detail in his
notes. We can imagine the sight: before dawn, darkened
building, silent guards, and then this luxurious conference
room, fully lit, windowless, filled with maps and filing
cabinets, several telephones of different colors. He was
greeted by three men: they were General Wynn Squash,
a military scientist whom we know directed the first
chain-reaction experiments in Chicago in 1942; Walter
Ratingen, advisor to the President; and Emory Wear, the
head of the CIA.

"They lost no time in explaining the reason for the
call, the overwhelming importance for secrecy. Einblick
noted in his record that, at the outset of the briefing, he
asked that a telephone line be opened to the Cobalt Clock
Laboratory in Nova Scotia, which calculated world-time
*precisely*; he was looking ahead to the *Horary timing of*

*the question*, to the precise moment when he was to understand his role, astrology's role in the crisis.

"They explained that a new weapon was on the verge of being used to end the War, that it was an atomic weapon, releasing enormous energy through the fission of radioactive elements. Einblick was a physicist as well. He understood their explanations and the briefing went swiftly.

"For us, it is important to understand just one point: in splitting an atom a particle is fired into the nucleus of an atom and is captured by the nucleus. In this case, more mass is added to the atom, and it is converted into a heavier element. Uranium 235 was used, but the amount of this U 235 in a given sample of Uranium is so small that a man-made substitute-synthesis had to be discovered. Scientists fired a neutron into a U 238 atom; it became trapped in the nucleus, forming the isotope U 239, which emits an electron forming Neptunium, which in turn emits an electron to form Pu 239, *Plutonium*. Plutonium will undergo fission just as U 235 does. This was man's first self-made element and permitted the scope of supply for the new weapon, the Atomic Bomb.

"The men explained that Plutonium   was being created in a secret laboratory in Charlottesville, Virginia, and was being transported to Oak Ridge, Tennessee, by truck. It was the highest secrecy maneuver possible. Two men were driving the medium-sized, highly insulated truck, very innocent-looking on the outside . . . but carrying inside it, in an enormous lead safe filled with a fluid suspension, a Plutonium supply *essential* to the bombs that would end World War II.   But the truck was long overdue, lost, maybe incredibly hijacked!

"The men said it quite bluntly and directly to Einblick: 'Where is the truck, the Plutonium. What has happened to it?' —Instantly, Einblick understood the question and grabbed the open line to the Nova Scotia Time Library: the constant time signal with voice synchronization pinpointed the time at exactly 10 hours, no minutes, no seconds, Greenwich Mean Time, standard. This checked with the watches in the room: General Squash had 6:02; Ratingen had 6:01; Wear, 6:00; and Einblick himself, 6:00:35. It was 10 in Greenwich, standard time—although England was on Double Summer Time then—the Cobalt Clock recorded only absolute standard time—and 6 in Washington, and since Washington was on War Time at the time, the time for horoscope timed to exactly 5:00 AM, Eastern Standard Time.   Einblick's role in the Manhattan Project had begun. In silence, he constructed the Horary Chart. (The slide screen was illuminated with the Chart.)

"Einblick must have been amazed at the first glance! We know how, in judging a Horary Chart, we need certain conditions, but they don't concern us here. The conditions *are* met: the Moon is *not* Void of Course; it makes several aspects before leaving the Sign; the Ascendant is *not* in the first or last five degrees of the Sign. And Einblick surely must have felt supreme confidence as he began to study the Ascendant, the Querent: the Sun was just above the Ascendant *only 61 minutes from the Ascendant degree of the United States*, in the chart we all use, drawn for 2:13 AM, July 4, 1776, Philadelphia, Ascendant 7 Gemini 35.

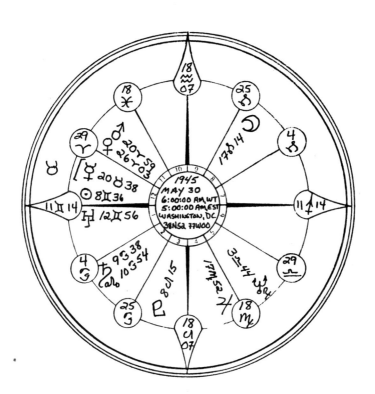

Just one degree separated the Horary Sun and the national Ascendant! And the Sun was exactly in the same degree and Sign as the US Uranus, and the Horary Uranus was in the same relative position, one degree below the Ascendant! The chart HAD TO BE VALID!"

The audience was on the edge of their seats.

"In fact, the cuspal arrangement throughout the Horary figure was almost exactly . . . to degree and Sign . . . what the cuspal arrangement is in the US Chart. It was as if the nation itself were sitting before Einblick and his chart.

"Now let's pretend that *we* were at the meeting too. Each of us is Einblick. We know that Mercury will rule the truck, the IIIrd rules truck drivers, the IXth rules interstate travel . . . Virginia to Tennessee. The Mercury rules the Ascendant, the Sun Sign, part of the XIIth and the Vth, speculation, and was itself intercepted in the XIIth: *the truck had indeed been intercepted*! That is immediately clear. The truck is somehow, somewhere being held in confinement!

"We know that we must check the aspects made by the Moon previous to the Horary moment to see what could have just transpired . . . and, here, it will be very important since the Moon is always co-ruler of the Querent, and rules the IInd, the national resources, and the IIIrd, the truck driver.

"The Moon has made an opposition with Saturn in the IInd, $7^\circ$ 36' earlier. This would have been the obstacle: the Moon-Saturn opposition from the VIIIth to the IInd. Einblick notes that he stopped on this point for quite some time and formulated three questions: they were 'why was transportation done by truck? what was the route of the trip? and what would be the average speed of the truck?'

"The CIA Director answered the questions. Wear said that a truck was used because of the radioactive danger of the Plutonium. Insulation weight and accident-potential factors had advised against air travel. The anonymity of a truck was a plus factor, certainly with more personal attention than on a train. And, indeed the two drivers, though checked-out, trustworthy, and highly experienced, knew nothing of their cargo: the van was completely sealed by welding. The drivers knew it was an important trip. They had made such trips before and had learned not to ask questions. They took command of the truck at a private warehouse in Charlottesville and began the trip at 6:00 AM on May 29. The speed governor on the truck allowed a maximum speed of only 35 miles-per-hour. The drivers ate and slept in the moving van and, considering short rest and fuel stops, the average was 27 miles-per-hour. The trip was a total of 550 miles to the depot southwest of Oak Ridge.

"Now, of course, Einblick was computing the occurrence of the Moon opposed Saturn. The 'confrontation' would have taken place 7° 36' by Moon motion *before the moment of his Horary figure*, this chart here. Einblick knew that the trip had been programmed for 20½ hours. Translating the Moon's motion of 7½ degrees *back* to the opposition with Saturn in the normal way, one degree every two hours, would have given the opposition, the 'trouble' 15 hours earlier. He asked another question.

He asked how they had checked the route and progress of the truck. It was inconceivable that they would not follow the truck somehow.

"CIA Director Wear said that cars followed the truck in shifts of 100 miles each, and they had indeed received an alarm from one of the trackers. But—now listen to this! —they wanted to test Einblick's work; they wondered if he could tell them when the alarm was given!

"Einblick records in his notes that he thought this was fair, and that it didn't unnerve him. He figured that, had the alarm come 15 hours ago, they would certainly have called him earlier or done something else radical to locate the shipment. His experience had shown him that often, for no explainable reason, the Moon's motion could be translated directly $1^{\circ}$ to 1 hour. This seemed more likely here . . . and another observation came to his gaze as he studied the chart and map of the region: the opposition would have taken place to the northeast of Oak Ridge, because of the IInd House Quadrant and the Cancer Sign. Some 7½ hours earlier, the truck would have been about 150 miles northeast of Oak Ridge . . . perhaps in Bristol, Tennessee, on the border of Virginia.

"Einblick tested that theory. He stated outright that the alarm could have come at 3:00 PM the preceding afternoon or—and more likely in his opinion—seven and one-half hours earlier at 10:30 or 11:00 PM the night before, May 29th. He suggested that the alarm could have come from the vicinity of Bristol, Tennessee.

"Well, can you imagine what happened in that room? It exploded! Einblick was absolutely right! All three men confirmed that the car tracking the truck just north of Bristol had been rammed by another car, quite severely, and could not go further. An agent had called the alarm number to report he had lost contact with the truck at 10:35 PM!

"Einblick still had work to do. He noted that every planet crossed into different houses before leaving the respective Signs. Here could be an emphasis on 'borders' geographically as well . . . and Bristol was a border city. As he pondered complex hierarchies of rulerships, two suddenly struck him: Saturn and the VIIIth House both rule *insurance*, and that was where the trouble was, where it had started.  He looked further: the Moon at that moment . . . the Horary moment . . . was into a Grand Trine in the Earth family with Jupiter and the vital Mercury. The truck was certainly in good hands, was safe, was 'practically self-sufficient.' But the truck and the drivers were, had been intercepted, and were being  institutionally held . . . judging from the XIIth House activity.

"There *would* be problems in six hours or so when the Moon would make a square with Mars in Aries. Einblick remembered feeling this 'heat' quite literally in his empathy with the chart. He saw the Sun as the authority symbol, also Uranus as ruler of the 'authority Xth.' The Plutonium was also safe in its sextile through Pluto to the Sun and Uranus . . . and it was in the 'transit' IIIrd.  He noted the square from Saturn to Neptune, but it was well past. Pluto and Mars ruled Scorpio intercepted in the VIth; Mars was still in a conjunction with Venus, ruler of the Libra part of the VIth and Taurus which held Mercury, the truck.

"Einblick's fantastic mind for synthesis put the facts together in his notes: the truck had been intercepted at the border by the police for insurance reasons. Truck and drivers had been detained. They knew only a train-depot destination. The police couldn't check them out. The police would begin to inspect the truck. Breaking the welded seals, they would come in contact with and expose the Plutonium!

"I can almost hear Einblick explaining all this. In his notes, he mentioned that it was at this point that common sense took over: he told the men that the truck had probably triggered an over-weight meter at the border check and had been detained by the police in Bristol for license-plate and insurance problems or inadequacies with regard to the weight of the load. The police had become suspicious of the men because of their lack of knowledge about the cargo and the thoroughly welded seals on the van. The official guard car was strangely not on the scene to explain. Somehow it too had been taken off course by accident or traffic. It was late at night, so the men were jailed and the truck impounded. Today was Memorial Day, a national holiday; surely it would be late in the day before the police could assemble welders and craftsmen to open the truck forcibly. There was still time.

"The story is fantastic! Both Wear and Ratingen went into an adjoining office to contact agents in Bristol and regain the truck. General Squash phoned the Pentagon and the White House about the lead. They all waited about 25 minutes, when Ratingen and Wear returned, their faces wreathed in smiles and triumph. Einblick had been absolutely right! The truck had been discovered in Bristol, with the State Police there, was still intact, had been released, and was on its way again to Oak Ridge, back together with the accompanying car."

The audience applauded!

"This is quite an example of astrology's service to the nation, ladies and gentlemen. The government was extremely grateful to Einblick, of course. They paid him handsomely for his work and also constructed a modest memorial to him: the guard-rail inside the apex of the Washington Monument. Look closely when you visit it next time: the rail is decorated with symbols of Pluto. It's really an appropriate memorial for Einblick high up in the tower, *in sight* of the Capitol."

There was a terrific applause . . . for the story and for the pun. The questions came fast and furiously, and I spent another 30 minutes answering as best as I could. It was a great evening.

As Mrs. Archer saw me to the cab that was to take me to the airport she was most cordial "We think it's amazing how that Mr. Aahnblick knew that England was on Double Summah Taahm at that taahm! If he hadn't, everything would've been off, wouldn't it?"

"You really got the point, Mrs. Archer. Sayonara!"

## Chapter Five

*CASE OF THE CUT-RATE PREDICTION*

It was terribly cold! No snow yet, but a dampness and a wind that were unbearable. I practically ran from the subway to my office building, grabbed the *Times* from Sam—even he was in his stall with two heaters—and couldn't wait to get some coffee. Cally always had it ready.

"Good morning, Merk."

"Good morning, Cally. I'm freezing. Any calls?"

"Nope, everything's on schedule so far," Cally reassured me. Every morning, I expected crisis. My office was perhaps the most unusual astrology office in the world.

I hung up my coat . . . I loved that Cashmere coat . . . Saville Row, London, vacation last Summer, but even *it* didn't keep out this New York rawness. And my gloves . . . my fingers were red, almost numb. Where can you find gloves that really work?

71

"Cally, bring in the mail and some coffee, lickety-split."

"Commmmmin' up, Merk!"

Cally brought in the mail. There was always a lot of mail now, since my book was published. People had such fantastic comments about what I wrote. I must receive 40 or 50 letters a month about my "Case of the Missing Moon." People miss the point. They look up the date of that case in the ephemeris and don't see things the way I saw them. Then they write to me for further explanation. If they didn't get it from my book, maybe they should go back to school. But it *was* nice to be published, to get those responses. Some were really beautiful . . . that lady who had been in Rumania and looked up the Yuga birth information in the Moon case . . . . she thought she had confirmation and was thrilled. I'd like to see that, learn more about it. I must write to her.

"Thank you, Cally." She had brought in the coffee and about 20 letters. We sat on the sofa. About eight of the envelopes contained bills; three or four were from clients travelling; and the rest were reactions to my book.

"Cally, I should never have published my own horoscope in the book. I guess it was a bow to egoism, but some of these people with so little knowledge it seems . . . they write in to give *me* advice. Lord knows I *need* it sometimes, but all astrologers should learn when *not* to offer advice.   Here, look at this." I handed Cally quite a lengthy letter.

"That's about 10 or 12 pages about *me*, Cally. Imagine that . . . this person . . . this Weaver Seenought in . . . in

Spokane," I looked at the return address on the envelope, He's really gone overboard. Read it through for me will you?" I handed Cally the many pages and the envelope.

The *Times* wasn't even warm yet. Brrr. Persephone's Almanac had said January 1973 would be para-normal. And Christmas had been almost balmy! Then, bang! New York's latitude had increased about 20 degrees!

"Merk," Cally asked gently, "you better look at this more carefully."

"What? That Spokane letter? Really? Let me have it."

I read through the first four or five pages very quickly. Sure enough, he had captured quite a bit of me from my horoscope: the Sun-Mercury conjunction in Gemini, the Capricorn Ascendant, Moon in Leo. He understood the public pull of the Moon intercepted in the VIIth, the creativity of the Sun-Mercury in the Vth. Thanks for the compliment, Mr. Seenought, I thought He covered the Taurus Uranus in the IVth, square the Moon, and the Saturn-Neptune opposition II-VIIIth. And, for the mid-heaven Jupiter in Scorpio . . . . thanks again, Mr. Seenought! . . . . you're right. Then, in the last pages:

*And Mr. Mercury, I must bring this to your attention. I thought of telephoning you. But you probably wouldn't even hear me out. I hope my writing this letter proves a bit to qualify my prediction: I fear for you on January 4th, in a few days, at 10:43 AM, New York time. As you know very well, there is a New Moon eclipse of the Sun over New York at that time in 14 Capricorn, exactly conjunct your Ascendant.*

Of course I was aware of this, but who in the world *really* understood Eclipse transits anyway. My goodness, for every time that predictions had been made that the world would crack open or stand still or do a flip-flop, I would like to have 10 bucks. I'd be rich. There was all that panic about the Mars-Saturn transit conjunction last spring. April, 1972, right *on* my Sun. No catastrophe. Hell, my book was published under that transit! It couldn't have been better. That's the trouble with a little bit of knowledge: panic, pessimism, expecting the worst. And now, *I'm* on the couch. This guy could've gotten my personality info from any number of synthesis cook-books. And now a prediction . . . and I wouldn't have to pay for it . . . . "Cut-rate!" I continued reading:

At the same time, there is a conjunction of Mars and Neptune at 3 Saggitarius  —he didn't even spell it right—opposed your Sun-Mercury from the XIIth House. Since this is approaching the Eastern horizon and because of the nature of Gemini and the other measurements that follow with this letter, I must caution you: I *fear that you will lose your left hand at this time*. I think you will lose it through your relationship with friends, your hopes, wishes, plans, or educational or publishing activities.

Absolutely preposterous. My *left* hand . . . the stock jargon about hopes and wishes and friends. What about my "hidden enemies?"   And the arithmetic . . . not mathematics . . . the arithmetic that followed!! Holy smokes! It looked like advanced cuneiform tablets: paragraph after paragraph of infinitesimal Directions and Pre-Natal Epoch measurements. It must have taken him a month! But all the same answer: I lose my left hand at 10:43 AM, January 4!! Preposterous. Cut-rate indeed!

HEY! THAT'S TODAY!! January 4 is today. My left hand's going to be cut-off or something in . . . in—I looked at my watch—in exactly one hour and twenty-three minutes!

"Cally, this is incredible!!! Absolutely incredible!" We both howled as we finished our coffee, and Cally cleaned up and went back to her office.

Amazing. Really, how presumptuous! The letter had been delayed in the holiday rush. Maybe I should call this guy at 10:43. It'd be 7:43 in Spokane. Maybe I'd get him out of bed, make him a bit uncomfortable . . . no, he'd be off to work. They start early out there. But how could I call him with one hand . . . and in the trauma of pain? Pain would come with it, wouldn't it? I laughed.

I stuffed the letter into my bottom drawer and put my desk in order.

Cally buzzed: "Merk, Gloria Canta, the opera singer is on the line."

"Thanks Cally, I'll take it." I switched lines: "Buon' giorno, diva divina, how'd it go?"

Gloria—really an American from Scranton—had just made a big debut at LaScala. She'd come to me before her trip, and we determined that everything was going in her favor. She was a Capricorn with a perfect Jupiter transit on her Sun at the time . . . last week.

"Merko, caro, you were right. It was a great triumph, triumfale magnifico!"

"I had nothing to do with it, Gloria; you deserved the hand!" The reference sounded strange in my ear. I meant applause, of course, and that's how you say it . . . but, after that letter, it *did* sound strange.

"And what a hand I got, Merk, seven bows . . . and a return contract!"

"That's great. Now you be sure to come check with me before the next trip, OK?" I teased her.

"Assolutamente! You're more important than my voice teacher!" she laughed . . . . that thousand dollar laugh . . . *per* laugh! "I called just to say thank you and tell you you're a 'dear.' "

"Thank you, diva; call again soon."

That was nice. Refreshing. Some life those singers live, country to country . . . the pressure.

Cally buzzed again: "Merk, do you want me to pay today's bill collection right away or wait until the end of the month?"

"Cally, we better do it today. Bring in the checks right away. Who knows? I might not be able to sign them after 10:43!"

We both were laughing again. "But Merk, you're not left-handed!"

"I know, but I think I'd be pretty darn uncomfortable for a while at least, don't you?" More laughter.

I took a glance at Mrs. Speertrager's chart. She'd be here at 11:00. This would be tough. The problem with her children. If she'd only kick that hyper-critical fussiness.

Virgo Sun-Neptune conjunction. Tough, the way it was configurated here. Cally came in.

"Here's the checkbook; and while you were on the phone, Mrs. Speertrager called and asked if we could make it for 1:00 today instead of 11:00. She was called into the school to pick up her son, just as you predicted. More trouble. I said we'd make the shift for her."

"Again? They make their lives so difficult, those people. She blames everyone else under the Sun . . . including the stars. OK. What do we have?"

Cally handed me the book and the bills.

"And while I'm doing this, would you mind moving those chairs back into position. Last night's conference ended too late for me to fix up. Thank you. You're awfully *handy* to have around." That last one was on purpose. I wanted to see if she was thinking about my pending doom.

"Clever, clever. Did he also write in that profile that I've got the cleverest man north of the Equator for a boss and astrologer?" We were really becoming silly, giggling.

The phone rang again . . . busy morning: "Michael Mercury."

"Good Morning, Merk," it was Evan Isis, my publisher. "Listen, the plans are just about set for your promo trip to the coast. Can you come over soon to go over some details with us? There's a tie-in we'd like to make in San Diego, with regard to the Paranormal Psychology Convention that's slated there for early March."

"I'd like to, Evan, but I'm tied up at eleven . . . no, that's been postponed . . . " I thought for a moment: "Sure I can. I can come over right away . . . a little after 10?"

"Fine; couldn't be better. We really want you to have a hand in these arrangements. We want you to be comfortable, not running around all over the place. It's a busy schedule."

"That's nice of you, Evan. You've done a great job on the book, and I'm really grateful. Gotta hand it to you! I'll be right over."

Funny, how normal conversations take on strange overtones when certain awarenesses are juggled into prominence. A couple more references to "hand." The suggestibility of man! Everybody, not just astrologers, has got to be really careful with words. We're all hypnotists in a way. It's like learning to use a new word . . . a word like "incongruous" or "indomitable" . . . . suddenly, the awareness that everyone around you is using it, and each time you hear it, it sounds like thunder! This guy Seenaught probably feels the same way about a few isolated astrology aspects he's picked up in some airport paperback! . . . but then again, he sure knows his arithmetic!

"Cally, I'm going down to Revelation Press; that was Isis; we're finalizing the coast trip. I'll be back by 12:30 for sure."

I was already dreading the cold again, grabbed my coat, moving quickly—I guess to get the circulation speeded up—caught the elevator right away, and crashed the cold barrier outside. It was two blocks over and three down. The walk would do me good, if my lungs could take the air! Certainly it'd be faster than a cab at that hour. So I started in, at a Harry Truman pace . . . and it really wasn't as bad as I'd thought . . . kind of invigorating.

I got to Revelation at 10:10, no doubt about it: the front of the building had that tricky Sun-dial Phoenix clock, Revelation's trademark, smack on the front of the building above the door. It wasn't too aesthetic, but it made the point . . . the point of Revelation Press: "the time for man has come." The 'hands' of time, I thought.

The escalator took me up to the mezzanine; then the elevator up to Evan's ninth floor suite. Now I was almost too warm. "I should walk that fast that far more often," I resolved. I felt great. Even my hands were warm. . . .

Then I thought about the prediction again. It was 10:15 or so now, a half-hour to go . . . . Evan wants me to give him a hand . . . my hands were warm . . . . but I hadn't worn my gloves . . . had forgot . . . but —and I felt into my pockets for my gloves— but where were they . . . where was it. . . . As I walked into Evan's outer office, I was still looking for the other glove. I couldn't find it . . . it must've dropped out on my way over.

"Good morning, Mr. Mercury," the receptionist said, "Mr. Isis is expecting you."

"Yes. Fine . . . uh . . . " - I hung up my coat on the chrome rack in the corner . . . "might I call my office first before I go in?"

"Certainly, Mr. Mercury," and she dialed my number and gave me the phone.

"Good morning, Michael Mercury's office." I heard Cally's voice.

"Cally, Merk. I'm at Revelation . . . and, I'm not kidding, now, but one of my gloves is lost!"

Cally caught on right away: "Which one, Merk?"

"The *left* one!"

Neither of us knew if one should laugh. I broke the silence: "Cally, the least we can do is write Mr. Seenought and correct his error: he was 28 minutes late!"

We both hung up in laughter. It was getting out of hand!

... *"I think the poem describes the hope of a birth, the trauma of a birth ..."*

## Chapter Six

### *THE CASE OF CASEY'S CRISIS*

It was Sunday afternoon. Cally and I were laying tiles on our waiting room floor. We enjoyed doing it ourselves and, with the waiting list for carpenters and floor-men these days, we could get the job done faster ourselves . . . and have some fun as well! I'm handy with my hands.

We were just about finished. It looked great: dark maroon tiles in a diagonal arrangement with dark gold. The sofa and side chairs were dark blue and the draperies white. Warm and comforting. I went into my office at the back. Cally was bringing in some cokes.

"Merk, now that I've got you to myself," she said as she put down the tray, ". . . and the phone won't ring, and you don't have any appointments, and you're tired, and . . ."

I knew what she was leading up to: our occasional

astrology lesson. She was coming along just fine, well enough to make most of my charts for me.

"OK, OK, Cally, you've got me. What'll we talk about today?"

"Merk, last Thursday, the Thursday before last, on Thanksgiving, I had dinner with my sister and her family. After dinner I read some stories to Jane and Josh just before they went to bed. One of the things I read them was *Casey at the Bat*. Do you remember that poem, by Ernest Lawrence Thayer?"

*Everybody* remembers that poem, I thought; the lines went through my mind, the ones I remembered from Junior High. It was a bad day for the Mudville nine, or something like that . . . Mighty Casey has struck out. Three strikes in *any* ball-game and you were out! "Of course, Cally, everybody remembers ol' Casey."

"Well, I thought I spotted something. And I studied the poem carefully for several days. I even went to the library to find out something about Thayer's life, and Merk, if you promise not to think I'm off my rocker, I want to show you what I've found."

"Fine, Cally," I humored her. Being named after one of Jupiter's moons was just perfect for her lofty enthusiasm. Let's hear it."

"OK." And she took out a sheaf of papers from the magazine rack. (She had this presentation totally planned!) "Here's a copy of the poem. Please read it through first, so you can remember more of it . . . and note that it has *52 lines*."

She said the last bit with emphasis. So what? Fifty-two lines. I read it through. Marvelous. That was America for you. The nostalgia. Certainly makes modern glass-architecture, television, supermarkets all look like institutions from another world. This *was* America . . . its spirit, its dust, hopes, its . . . I was really carried away too.

Cally interrupted: "Now, I think Thayer was saying something much more here than the crisis of a baseball game, the fall of a local hero."

"I do too, Cally. He's writing about the energies of an era . . . nostalgia, something everyone can identify with, the young history of America, the birth of hope and . . ."

"Oh, Merk, you're fantastic. You've got it! You've seen what I see: the birth of hope . . . the hope of birth. You're amazing!"

I was a bit uneasy with her compliment. I didn't feel profound at all. In fact, I was kind of worn out. My knees were beginning to hurt from all that floor work.

"Merk, I think Thayer's poem describes the hope of a birth, the trauma of a birth within a very sad family. The baby comes, 'strikes out,' if you will, dies; the joys are gone. Merk, I think this poem is AS-TRO-LO-GI-CAL!"

By this time, it was clear that Cally had gone off the . . . a deep end.

"Really now, Cally, it's just a poem of nostalgia and a kind of patriotism. It couldn't possibly be so filled with meanings; why, others would have . . . "

"But Merk, you said it yourself: 'the birth of hope' . . ."

"But I talk in those symbols all the time; it was an accident . . ."

"So do poets."

"Granted, but . . . "

"No. Please let me finish . . . you promised."

She was right. I stopped defending I-don't-know-what, and I decided to enjoy the entertainment.   "OK, Cally, you're up!"

She smiled: "I went to the library, as I said, and I found just a teeny bit about this poet Thayer. He was born in Western Pennsylvania in 1872. He was a Sagittarian. And the little biography mentioned that he was born at 5:45 AM! Now, *that's* highly unusual! It told me that Thayer was definitely interested in astrology. Nobody in the New World at that time knew much about astrology. Everyone was recovering from the Civil War, but he became interested in astrology when he was older and obviously found out his birth time somehow."

"So you have Thayer's horoscope."

"No. The town he gave as his birthplace doesn't exist anymore, and I haven't had the time to write to Harrisburg to find out exactly where it was. No; I have his poem. —Now, please listen Merk: I further found out from the short biography that Thayer had had a very unhappy life. He had several children who died shortly after birth . . . the mortality rate was so high then . . . and a son who was convicted as a thief . . . and the son was shot during an escape from a Pittsburg prison. Thayer then moved to Connecticut, lived like an hermit, and wrote poetry. He died in obsurity in 1926 at 54.

"Now, I think the poem 'Casey at the Bat' *is a poem*

*about his son.*

"And you see all this in the poem, Cally?" I asked gently.

"Yes. Let me show you." There was no stopping her eagerness. "The title itself shows his son taking his turn in life . . . 'Casey at the Bat.' The biography I read was written long after Thayer had written the poem and there was no mention of the son's name. But, whether it was 'Casey' or not . . . and it could have been . . . Thayer was describing a young sturdy male taking a 'swing' in life. Stepping up to life's responsibilities and striking out.

"The first two lines tell us the son's birth Sign and the time of birth,"

Cally leaned forward with me and read the lines aloud, pointing at each word with the pencil:

*'It looked extremely rocky for the Mudville nine that day*
*The score stood two to four with but an inning left to play.'*

"The son—let's call him 'Casey'—Casey was a Capricorn . . . rocky, mud, etc. and was born between one and two in the afternoon: I get that from the nine . . . the ninth House . . . the Capricorn ninth . . . and, in the second line: two to four plus one—one inning—equal nine . . . and there are nine innings in the game. That's really clear to me, Merk.

"Now, I think the next four lines describe the fear that surrounded Casey's birth. Several of Thayer's children had died at birth and as youngsters. Giving birth was traumatic for Mrs. Thayer. Here, read further:

*'So when Cooney died at second and Burrows did the same'*—these were common boys' names then. These children died at two, after difficult births.

> *A pallor wreathed the features of the patrons of the game.*

The parents . . . certainly the 'patrons' . . . were afraid about Casey's birth. The 'wreath' in 'wreathed' certainly means horoscope. They were afraid in their horoscopes, and the fear and trauma would be in Casey's horoscope as well. We've seen that many times right here in this office, Merk.

> *A straggling few got up to go, leaving there the rest
> With that hope which springs eternal within the human breast.*

"The friends of the family had given up hope and gone. The mid-wife stayed on, of course . . . and what a beautiful mother-fortitude image there, 'that hope which springs eternal within the human breast.' Beautiful!"

I really was amazed. Cally was making sense. She continued:

> *For they thought, if only Casey could get a whack at that;*
> *They'd put even money now with Casey at the bat.*

Here the birth was proceeding. Hope was present. Casey may even have been named before the birth . . . that's often the case . . . oops, sorry Merk, I didn't mean that as a pun . . . and 'at the bat,' as we've seen, means a chance at life.

"These next two lines describe two of Casey's living brothers:

> *But Flynn preceded Casey and likewise so did Blake,*
> *And the former was a puddin' and the latter was a fake.*

Flynn was a 'puddin',' a softy, and Blake was undoubtedly adopted or taken over from some other family killed in an Indian raid or something.

> *So on that stricken multitude a death-like silence sat,*
> *For there seemed but little chance of Casey's getting to the bat.*

Here Thayer reminds us of the great problem surrounding birth in those days. The hope of the birth was slim . . . but . . . fervent.

"There must have been a crisis at the birth moment. These next lines suggest how the whole family was brought into play, how the two brothers really showed their stuff:

> *But Flynn let drive a single to the wonderment of all,*

*And the much despised Blakey tore the cover off
the ball!*
*And when the dust had lifted and they saw what
had occurred,*
*There was Blakey safe at second and Flynn a-
hugging third.*

I think Mrs. Thayer may have been hemorrhaging. I
think Flynn single-handedly ran for the doctor in the vil-
lage, and Blakey tore open a ball of cotton swabbing that
was used for rifles, and first-aid as well. Blakey became a
"second" to the mid-wife and Flynn returned with the
third party, the doctor:

*Then from the gladded multitude went up a joyous
yell—*
*It rumbled in the mountain tops; it rattled in the
dell;*
*It struck upon the hillside and rebounded on the
flat—*
*For Casey, mighty Casey, was advancing to the
bat!*

Now these lines are most, most important. They tell
so much: everyone was jubilant. It seemed that Casey
would make it. Then, we have this reference to opposition
with the birth Sun: it "rumbled in the mountain tops and
rattled in the dell." It sounds to me that Saturn or Mars
was opposing the Sun in Capricorn, near the mountaintop,
in Capricorn in the IXth.   And also, these are typical

poetical classical references . . . the gift of the gods, so to speak . . . from the mountains . . . Olympus . . . in the dell . . . the Delphic oracle. It's struck on the hillside . . . that's the Zenith-Nadir axis . . . and rebounded on the flat . . .THAT HAS TO BE THE HORIZON . . . the Ascendant. The traumatic opposition was square the horizon as well. And Casey was about to be born!!

Now, Merk, he was born *healthy*. Perfectly healthy. Read this:

> *There was ease in Casey's manner as he stepped into his place.*
> *There was pride in Casey's bearing and a smile on Casey's face.*

Here was the Capricorn bearing and pride, and I'm sure he had an Aries-Taurus Ascendant. It would fit the IXth House birth-time in Capricorn. The problem in the birth caused a feet-first delivery, but the smile would mean the safety of the delivery, the success of the birth."

"Go on." I said, "Continue." I was really engrossed with this. It really seemed clear to me too.

Cally continued: "Thayer reinforces this in the next two lines:

> *And when, responding to the cheers, he lightly doffed his hat,*
> *No stranger in the crowd could doubt: 'twas Casey at the bat.*

The "hat" is the placenta, most certainly. Casey had "stepped into his place."

Thayer, I think, now uses less detail and more of an over-view of his son's life, Casey's life, as it progresses:

> *Ten thousand eyes were on him as he rubbed his hands with dirt;*
> *Five thousand tongues applauded when he wiped them on his shirt.*

These were the early years. The child must have had considerable drive and, in the mistakes he made, the trouble he got into, he probably was admonished and given second and third chances. He was a special child. Everyone was watching his progress. "Wiping them on his shirt" seems to refer to owning up to things when he was caught, soiling the expectation of "uniform" behavior:

> *Then when the writhing pitcher ground the ball into his hip,*
> *Defiance glanced in Casey's eye, a sneer curled Casey's lip.*

This is very important, Merk. The "ball" is the Sun. The pitches coming up are progressed moments . . . important moments in the Sun's progression, the boy developing in time. Thayer is telling us that Casey hardened with maturity. Then:

> *And now the leather covered sphere came hurling through the air,*

> *And Casey stood a-watching it in haughty grandeur*
> *there.*
> *Close to the sturdy batsman, the ball unheeded*
> *sped;*
> *That ain't my style, said Casey. STRIKE ONE, the*
> *umpire said.*

It's perfectly clear here that Casey passed up opportunities, maybe golden ones. Maybe he was offered a practical job, maybe in a tannery . . . a Capricorn-Saturn occupation . . . and the reference to leather here . . . we can't be sure of that. But he passed it up and got into trouble; his first tangle with the Law, the umpire. Maybe his first time in jail. Thayer goes on:

> *From the benches black with people there went up*
> *a muffled roar:*
> *Like the beating of the storm waves on the stern*
> *and distant shore,*
> *Kill him, kill the umpire, shouted someone on the*
> *stand.*
> *And it's likely they'd've killed him had not Casey*
> *raised his hand.*

Casey was tried in a Court for his first offense . . . that's the reference to the 'benches black with people,' the judge or judges in black robes. Perhaps an accomplice on the witness stand exploded in defiance against the judge . . . but Casey still had some good in him, and he put down the storm . . . . . probably by raising his hand, swearing to tell the whole truth of the situation. That's probably how he got off with probation or something. At any rate, he got another chance. Thayer repeats this thought in the next four lines;

> *With a smile of Christian Charity, great Casey's visage shone;*

(and here could have been Moon in Leo with Jupiter in conjunction . . . I just 'feel' it, Merk)

> *He stilled the rising tumult, he made the game go on. He signalled to the pitcher and once more the spheroid flew,*

(Casey had a second chance in later years)

> *But Casey still ignored it and the umpire said STRIKE TWO.*

He did something else wrong . . . this time: fraud, I think . . . look, Thayer tells us:

> *Fraud, cried the maddened thousands, and the echo answered, Fraud.*
> *But one scornful look from Casey and the audience was awed:*
> *They saw his face grow stern and cold. They saw his muscles strain.*
> *And they knew that Casey wouldn't let the ball go by again.*

What heartbreak for Thayer! This son who had come into his life under such hopeful and traumatic circumstances was letting down the very hope that had given him life. He was becoming scornful of the world. He somehow defrauded lots of people . . . including his father . . . "wouldn't let the ball go by again" really means . . . must mean *couldn't* . . . it was inconceivable to Thayer, to all the people in the town, that Casey would fall again. But then, we can share Thayer's sorrow: look at these next lines, Merk:

> *The sneer is gone from Casey's lips, his teeth are clenched in hate.*
> *He pounds with cruel vengeance his bat upon the plate.*
> *And now the pitcher holds his ball, and now he lets it go*
> *And now the air is shattered by the force of Casey's blow.*

Notice how Thayer switches to the present tense here. He's almost describing an eternal Casey, the way he is now in terms of his end. The "sneer gone" and the "teeth clenched in hate": that could mean Casey's death in scorn and hate of the world, his face frozen before Thayer for eternity. Casey seems to have avenged himself against society in the time left to him. I think the "air shattered" refers to Casey's Midheaven, which would've been the Air Sign Aquarius . . . this we have already determined . . . it could refer to his Zenith of failure . . . his being shot in the escape attempt . . . fleeing, flying from captivity . . . a life, a dream shattered.

In the final stanzas, Thayer speaks of his despair to all the world . . . to all America, understanding so well the mysteries that bind us all:

> *Oh! somewhere in this favored land, the Sun is shining bright*

(he is reviewing life and giving a final clue with his word *Sun*)

> *The band is playing somewhere and somewhere hearts are light.*
> *And somewhere men are laughing and somewhere children shout.*
> *But there is no joy in Mudville: mighty Casey has struck out.*

These 52 lines . . . 52, Merk, because I think this was a kind of progressed symbolism, letting 52 lines . . . 52 weeks in the year . . . stand for a lifetime . . . these lines tell a powerful story of struggle and failure in life. And, in the edition I studied, there was a postscript added by an editor or someone . . . maybe even Thayer. It said "and we can be sure that Casey would redeem himself another day." It wasn't part of the poem, absolutely not, but it stated so beautifully the only rationale Thayer had: that Casey would redeem himself in another life.

Cally was finished. She stopped talking. We were

both silent, and her eyes were filled with tears.

"Let's have another coke, Cally," I said, giving her a chance to leave the room and regain her composure. The poem *was/is* quite moving, but we had gone through it in an extreme of symbolism, and we hadn't even mentioned baseball! My eyes covered the text again, quickly. Cally's thoughts were still *in* those lines . . . not the dusty cheers of a baseball crowd . . . but the anguish of a father's hope, destroyed by a wayward son . . . Cally herself had given birth to much more than a baseball game.

Cally came back in, smiling in a bit of embarrassment.

"Cally, I don't know what to say. It's amazing that you could get all of this out of those lines . . . astrologically or psychically . . . or just by sheer emotional imagination."

"Merk, I don't know how to say it, the feelings were so strong in me. I remembered how you always say that we should use our astrological awareness when we read books, see plays, and so on. I did just that, and a whole new world of meaning came to me."

I nodded. There was not much for me to say.

"I think I really am right," she continued poignantly.

"Well, there's no way we'll ever know. For any symbolic analysis, you need the client's corroboration. But, from my point of view, you've not made any errors," —we both grinned broadly—"and I see it as a rewarding exercise for you. I don't know how much was grounded on astrology. . . but, I would say," and here I was sounding professional for effect, "that for your thesis you had your native enthusiasm, feminine intuition, and a superb audience as your three bases!"

This time, we both laughed out loud.  It was dinner time.  Time to get home

*"And there I saw it, covered with vines and mosses . . ."*

## Chapter Seven

### CASE OF THE SOLDIER OF THE UNKNOWN TOMB

Cally ushered the officer through the office door: "Merk, this is Colonel Guard. Colonel, Michael Mercury."

The Colonel was impressive in his uniform that was neatly tailored to his wiry frame. His sand-colored hair was slightly disheveled, not because of the hasty removal of his braided uniform hat, but from his obvious rush to get to the office on time. His face was healthfully flushed, his chin appropriately pointed . . . the Aries Ascendant blended with the Gemini Sun totally clearly.

"Thank you, Cally. Colonel, Good morning; I was worried for you. Was there some last-minute complication?"

"Good morning, Mr. Mercury. Yes, I'm sorry to be so late. Fifteen minutes, is it?"

"Twelve! I start to give up at fifteen," I answered lightly.

"It's been the story of my life: running around non-stop. I guess you could predict that I'd be late for my own funeral!"

"Colonel, I understand. Geminis have that tendency. But please sit down and be comfortable. We can easily catch up with the schedule."

The Colonel adjusted his position in the dark brown leather chair set before my desk, and I began to see how he built a protection wall around himself. Even his being late was a kind of defense, perhaps not wanting to face up to relationships. Venus ruling his VIIth completed his enormous Aries Ego thrust with the Moon-Mars conjunction in the Ascendant and made two squares, to Uranus and Neptune. Here were the two worlds again, one intensely individual, the other diffident, perhaps private. The eastern orientation of the horoscope was a clear ego-defense structure.

"Don't be on guard, Colonel, if you'll excuse that multiple pun . . ."

Colonel Guard smiled. I was trying to put him at ease, to get his attention; something was bothering him. The time was late, so I decided to begin directly with the heart of the consultation . . . however that would be conceived by Colonel Guard: "Colonel, why are you here today? What's bothering you?"

The Colonel's eyes were directed to his shining Cordovan shoes, specifically to the heel of his left foot resting crossed on his right knee. The fingers of his right

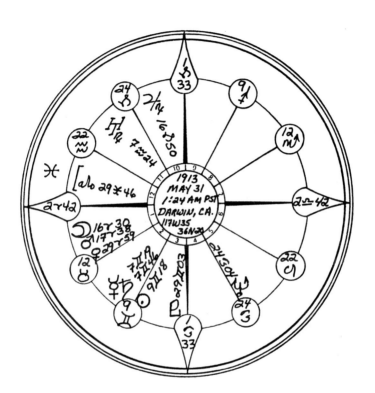

hand played nervously with his left trouser cuff. He spoke haltingly, still evading confrontation with my eyes: "Mr. Mercury . . . I guess . . . I guess you could say I have an important career choice to make." Only upon completion of his sentence did his eyes meet mine, and then, as quickly, they moved back to his left heel.

"I see that.".

The measurements were very clear: we were together this day, one week after the Colonel's 61st birthday, and transiting Mars and Saturn were in conjunction precisely upon his fourth cusp. That gave a Solar Arc measurement of 58 degrees and 13 minutes, bringing the Sun to exact opposition to natal Uranus and the Midheaven to a trine with Pluto, which natally squared his Ascendant. Here indeed was a new start for personal projection through job perspective.

I continued: "It's clear astrologically, but first may I ask just exactly what is your work now. Of course, I know you are in the military, but what exact work do you . . . "

The Colonel interrupted my question. He smiled his words directly to me, as if sharing a life-long charade: "I write textbooks for government agencies and particular industries. They begin as world-wide research projects and end up as textbooks. They deal with two fields: sociology and industrial conversion . . . these two dimensions within historical change."

"That's quite a specialty. Would you elaborate please?"

"Well, it's all a deadly bore, but I got into this at the close of World War II. You know, studying the population revival and adjustments throughout Europe and the Far East. I guess my major themes involve how populations respond to current events and how industry adapts to change. They do get inter-related, but as I said, it isn't very exciting."

"It *is* complex, Colonel. *That* I can appreciate. But it has brought you security, fame, appreciation; a full career."

"Sure it has. I guess you're going to tell me how important ego recognition is to me, the diversity, the moving around . . . "

"You know some astrology!"

"My wife's got a lot of those glossy magazines around. I've snuk a peek or two!" And the Colonel showed a trace of humor, as well as the press of curiosity. But still his gaze was upon his feet more than it ever was on me. He had shifted position now, so that his right heel was upstaging me.

My eyes went to the powerful third House cusp area, noted the final dispositor of Mercury, the Plutonic significances with regard to sociology and demographics. All he told me was clear.

In order to let the Colonel rest his clear preoccupation, I started another line of questioning: "Colonel, you're born in Darwin, California. While waiting for you to arrive, I looked this up on the map: it's a tiny town very close to Death Valley!"

My ploy worked: the Colonel brightened, and his eyes held mine for the longest time yet. He continued with some real enthusiasm: "Right. Never met anyone born in Darwin before, have you?"

"No, I haven't!"

"Well, it's a hot, dusty place. It was then. My father worked as a guide on Telescope Peak; that's a straight shot east and up, some 11,000 feet up, right at the entrance to Death Valley."

"And Darwin is only 50 miles west of the lowest point in North America! My map said '282 feet below sea level!' "

"It sure is. My father used to say that his workday took him from the grave to the heavens!"

There was humor in our banter, but suddenly I became aware of the multiple references to "death" and connected concepts that had been buried in our conversation. Maybe *this* was Colonel Guard's preoccupation. Pluto squared his Ascendant and sextiled that Venus. Pluto ruled his VIIIth House in Scorpio. I approximated the Solar Arc of Pluto to conjunction with Neptune, adding a year because of the slow diurnal birth movement of the natal Sun.

Out of our light laughter, I resumed my questioning, and I leaned back in my large chair to take any possible threat out of inquiry, feeling certain that the nerve would be touched: "Colonel, please take your mind back to 1939. You were 26 years old." And here I quickly looked for 1939 on the abbreviated ephemeris pages under my glass desk top. I found that transiting Saturn had conjoined the Colonel's Moon in March, just before his 26th birthday, undoubtedly focusing that supernatual Pluto-Neptune Solar Arc. I leaned back again from my desk: "In the Spring, maybe March 1939."

The Colonel stopped fidgeting. He sat motionless. He paled. His eyes stayed diverted from mine.

I leaned forward consolingly, and chanced another deduction: "Might that time have a connection to the time about eight years earlier?" This was the Solar Arc square between Pluto and the Moon in 1931, when transiting Uranus was on the Moon and transiting Saturn on natal Jupiter, approaching opposition to natal Neptune. Additionally, Solar Arc Sun was conjoining natal Pluto. I added softly: "Did a parent, your mother perhaps, die in 1931, and is there a connection here with that time in the Spring of 1939?"

The Colonel looked up. Two lines of tears eased over his cheeks, and his face began to regain its color with the release of long held privacy. He spoke wistfully: "Mr. Mercury, she was a tender, tender soul. You're right on both counts: she died in May; May 14th, just before my 18th birthday. I was at the University of Minnesota in the Twin Cities, and I flew home for the funeral. She's buried in the Valley. She loved that land."

I worked to rescue the Colonel from his grief. "And the connection with spring 1939, eight years later?"

The Colonel looked at me long and hard. His tears stopped, and his eyes gave me total attention. He sat forward on his chair and whispered his private memory:

"At that time, I had gotten my PhD in Sociology, and I was bored with the work with the proletariat; you know, the assembly line problems of industry then. Sociologists were rare birds in those days, and their work was confined to blue-collar phenomena within our young technocracy. I joined the military. I had always wanted to be a soldier—and I guess that shows somewhere in my horoscope too."

"It does. The Aries dimensions are strongly militaristic. But you need a large framework for your work. The military, the government. It's obvious. The only danger would be that your own individuality would get lost within the big picture."

"Right. I fought that always. Anyway, as a child, I had always fantasized Indian battles in the Valley. Then I read every book I could get my hands on about World War I, but Ma had always balanced . . . that's a good word . . . balanced this with ideas about my becoming a professor. So the PhD was damn important to me. Well, I sort of put the two together, didn't I?" And here the Colonel laughed a bit, another stage of tension release.

He continued: "Well, I was in Italy early in 1939. I was there to study the public opinion climate with the rise of Mussolini and Fascism. I centered my work in Florence—I was only there for five months; things got hot very quickly—and what a place that was . . . what a memory."

Colonel Guard's thoughts began to drift. His voice was an echo of poignant recollections. I steered him back to the experience we both were searching for: "What about the Spring of 1939, specifically?"

"I don't know how to tell this, Mr. Mercury. Nobody really knows what went on. Sure there are hospital records—and I'm embarrassed still by them . . . but . . ."

"Please, Colonel, don't be embarrassed now. Just share the story with me."

"Well, I was taking a weekend off, and I set out on a long overnight hike to Fiesole, a small hill-town outside of Florence. Towards evening, I set up my tiny camp on the edge of a grove of olive trees. I felt totally isolated. It was very late in the long Spring afternoon, and no one was anywhere in sight. There were enforced political meetings in the towns, and the hillsides were desolate.

"You're not going to believe all this, Mr. Mercury . . ."

"Please, Colonel. I want to hear it. Just tell me the story."

"Alright; you asked for it. I started planning some sunset pictures, really a way just to appreciate that dry scenery, those twisted trees. And then I went into the tangled brush on the side of this little hill. I went in about . . . about thirty feet or so, looking for some good kindling wood for a small cooking fire—I had some veal, some green beans, and some wine and bread. And there I saw it, covered with vines and moss . . . it . . . was . . . it was so moving. That's the word: moving."

Colonel Guard paused and stared right through me. He was clearly recreating the image of what he saw, of what he had recreated probably thousands of times since that day in 1939.

"Yes, Colonel? What did you see?"

"I saw a tomb. A tomb. It was a sarcophagus, with its major length protruding from the earth and its whole girth wrapped in vines and caked with moss. The exposed limestone portions shone pink from the late afternoon sunlight that followed my path into the brush."

"Was there an inscription, any identification on the stone?"

"None . . . or I should say, a faint indication that had been worn away by time. Now, I know that Etruscan tombs dot the area—and, of course, I assume that this was one of them. They cause no stir among the people, and that's probably why it was undisturbed . . . I mean, the people honor these sites, build their farms around them, you understand?"

"Yes. But what else happened?"

"Well, Mr. Mercury, it amazes me that I can talk about this so . . . so comparatively easily now. There was a time when . . . when I simply could not do it. But I'm getting ahead of myself. Standing there studying the tomb, I became hypnotized; transfixed might be a better word. I had to open it. I simply had to. I tore myself away, went back to my back-pack and got my machete, my fox-hole shovel, and flashlight. I roared back to the tomb and started cutting the vines, scraping off the moss, loosening the earth around the sarcophagus. It took me almost an hour, but, somehow, I had the energy of several men. I was . . . well, later they called me a 'maniac'.

"Mr. Mercury, I succeeded in sliding aside the top portion of the lid. It had a crack in it, and perhaps my banging away increased it, but I finally got inside. And · . . And —"

Colonel Guard shifted his position, came even further forward in his chair toward me. He took the small glass of water I routinely had poured at the beginning of the interview, gulped it down and resumed his story quickly, urgently.

"And I saw nothing . . . nothing real, mind you— no mummy, no wood inner coffin or the like—but I saw . . . I saw my mother! Her face was inside the tomb!"

I worked hard not to jump at the revelation. The entire interview took a tremendous turn of focus. My silence elicited silence from him. I finally spoke: "Please, Colonel; what else?"

"Well, she spoke to me. She smiled and spoke to me. She said, *'Tod, my dear Tod, protect the grave and comfort the dead.'* She kept repeating and repeating that . . . that command, that request: 'protect the grave and comfort the dead'."

"How did you interpret that, Colonel?"

"I didn't know then. I still don't, and that's part of the reason I'm here with you, I guess. But the next thing I knew it was three days later. Some farmers found me unconscious upon that tomb. I . . I guess I had gone over the deep end, so to speak. The doctors back in Florence said I had had a nervous breakdown. I was shipped home—supposedly incoherent—to the Walter Reed Army Hospital. It took about three months to re-

cuperate, and . . and I had to fight like hell to keep that
so-called blemish off my record . . . or at least in the
proper perspective."

"And that was in March, 1939?"

"It was actually April 7th."

"Fine. Well, you were classically open to a super-
natural experience at that time. That was the basis for
my deductions and questions earlier. And it's perfectly
clear how it's linked to your mother's death a few years
earlier. Now, let me ask you about the significance of what
your mother said: was her grave in Death Valley in jeopar-
dy somehow?"

"Yes and no. There was a small struggle to get per-
mission to bury her where we did, but my father as a
guide there was able to get it arranged. A few prospective
claims threatened to violate the area, but for years there's
been nothing. No problem.

"I see what you're thinking, Mr. Mercury, but I feel
that she meant *generally* . . . you know, the general grave
. . . protect the symbolism of the grave and comfort the
principle of death, of the dead. That's . . . that's how I've
come to live with it all."

"I see. Have you done anything in those years now to
follow her . . . her command?"

"Right after the War, I went back to Italy and I
was able to buy the plot of land that holds that tomb.
The countryside was divided up after all the bombing,
and I secured that plot. I'm damn proud of that! I own
it still today. Put a little fence around it; made it look
. . . uh . . . private and . . . comfortable."

"Anything more?"

"No. Nothing more, but it bothers me."

"What does?"

"That I *should* be doing more, much more to protect the grave and comfort the dead. Help me, Mr. Mercury—if you can—I'm retiring this Summer and I want to devote my life to . . . to the dead. Can you understand that?"

"Colonel, Thomas Mann once said, 'A man's dying is more the survivors' affair than his own'. That says a lot, doesn't it?"

Colonel Guard was touched by the quote. I was stalling, my eyes studying the horoscope carefully in the light of everything that had been said. I made quick notes on my yellow pad as the Colonel philosophized about the survivors' roles in caring for the dead. His Moon and Mars conjunction made very close quintiles to his Pluto, now activated by the Mars-Saturn transit at the fourth cusp. Here was a creative management of death, at one level of symbolism, a finding of Ego through death. The writing focus of the Gemini and IIIrd House emphasis would have to give way also to another level of symbolism . . . and then it all came together in my mind!

"In general, Colonel, everything you've said is right here in the horoscope. Of course, it has specific meaning for you as an individual by the way you have reacted to all that has happened. But I have to say that you are now coming to grips with, really, a life's work."

"I feel that too, but it's kind of stupid, isn't it? I mean, my wife and I haven't really talked about this for years. I've had a great and adventurous career. Now what? What in the world can I do to fulfill that . . . that sentence?"

"Let me point out a few things to you: you were born on a Saturday; that's the day of Saturn, through legend and deduction the planet linked with graves, tombs, the dead. In your horoscope, Saturn rules your Midheaven, the place of profession, and it's in close conjunction with your Sun. You were born in Darwin, California; the name Darwin even has significance here in the life-death-life evolutionary sense. Even California in the West, the compass direction usually linked with death, because of the setting Sun. And, Colonel, even your first name, 'Tod'; it . . ."

"I know. 'Tod' in German means 'death'."

"Right! Look how all of this symbolism accumulates. It's incredible!"

"Yes, it is."

"Your father even said that you lived in the lowest spot in North America, its grave."

"Right."

"Now, Colonel, you work in the Pentagon, correct?"

"Yes."

"Right alongside Arlington Cemetery."

Excitedly, the Colonel jumped back in enthusiasm: "Yes! I often go over there during lunch-times. I jog. I jog through the grave areas on the southern bank. Actually along the southern perimeter, not actually among the graves."

"Colonel, I might sound absurd to you, but the symbols of the horoscope show the plausibility that you could enjoy life . . . as . . . as a tour guide in the national cemetery."

My words sounded ridiculous to my own ears, but to the Colonel they were revelatory. The third House had to speak: all the Mercury explosiveness.

"My God, Mercury! That's it! That's IT! And my *father* was a guide. It fits. I'd care for and comfort the dead!"

"You will have a fine pension, so financial security is no problem. You would be fulfilling your mother's command, and, if I may add, *your horoscope.*"

"Mr. Mercury, that's fantastic! God, I feel relieved somehow."

Colonel Guard took several deep breaths and sat back deeply into his chair.

"And there's another interesting quote about these subjects, which I'd like to share with you: Stalin said, 'A single death is a tragedy, a million deaths is a statistic.' You'd *soften* the latter."

The Colonel whistled in amazement.

"Dead on, eh Colonel?"

My words brought laughter back between us. I rose up and walked around to him, offering my hand.

"I thank you so, Mr. Mercury. It's simply amazing."

"Fine. Thank you, Colonel. Now, we haven't gone over the time schedule of your retirement. You are a little late with your plans, but I think there will be no major problems."

"No, there won't be. My wife may pass out when I tell her about all this, but she's a good sport; she'll see how happy it'll make me. After all, it'll just be a part-time job, but . . ."

I interrupted him, handing him his hat and offering a second handshake:

". . . but just enough to fulfill your vision, right?"

"Right you are. Thank you again."

I followed Colonel Guard out through Cally's reception room. He went swiftly through the door, his chin thrust forward, in eagerness and determination . . . and probably late for his next appointment.

"Cally, that was really something! Here, put his chart in his file, would you please?"

"Did you help him, Merk?"

"I'm sure I did. But it was bizarre, to say the least. I had to really get into his subconscious."

"Gee! What tipped you off?"

"He had this strange way of playing with his trouser cuffs, directing his eyes to his feet, and . . ."

"I got it! Neptune rules the XIIth, with Pisces intercepted, and Pisces rules the feet, and is the only planet in the eastern . . ."

"Well . . . I guess that's acceptable, but there's *so* much more."

"And did you have to get at his mother complex?"

Cally had prepared the chart and was surely familiar with it, but glib reference to the Colonel's mother aroused an over-reaction in me after what I had just been through. "How in the world do you know about his mother?"

"Well, remember your own words: 'When the nodal axis is closely configurated by conjunction or square with another planet, the maternal influence in terms of the aspecting planet is ENORMOUS'."

Cally was joshing me a bit, and I finally got back to the reality of her fun. "Right you are, crafty Cally. And here we've got Pluto squaring the nodal axis, right? Which is at the midpoint of Midheaven/Pluto, right?" And I pushed even further the fun: "And the Moon rules Cancer on the IVth and is square Neptune, RIGHT?"

"OK, Merk. It's always said several ways, right?" she backed off.

"Yes, Cally. His mother did dominate his whole life perspective, but in curious ways. I guess that *is* the Neptune part of it." And, in returning to my office, I couldn't resist trying to get the last word in our little sparring match: "But what would you have explored next, Miss Smartypants?"

"You win, chief. I would've come to a dead end!"

"Right. The real meaning of every horoscope is in the human being, not in the symbols."

*"The future is not entertainment."*

## Chapter Eight

*CASE OF THE THOUGHTFUL MENTALIST*

"Something just came to me, ladies and gentlemen. Let's try a quick little experiment. Alright?"

Zarnoff the Great moved to the very front lip of the Kennedy Center Opera House stage, just on the edge of his lighted area. The follow spot's intensity illuminated his tall, lean figure sharply, and the flood of blue klieg lights softened the rest of the stage supernaturally.

"All of you out there think of any number between . . . let's say . . . between 50 and 100. Alright? Good. Now let's tune our thoughts together: I'll guide your thoughts, and your thoughts will guide mine. Let's say the number must have two digits . . . let's say that the two digits must be even numbers . . . Got that? . . . and let's say that the two digits cannot be the same . . . they must be different. All right? Now concentrate hard on the number . . . and

*119*

send it to me. That's it . . . I'm getting it. Concentrate hard.

"Alright: I . . . get . . . EIGHTY-SIX or maybe it's SIXTY-EIGHT!!"

There was an immediate eruption of response from the vast majority of the audience. Astonished corroboration rippled through the sea of people and transformed itself into enthusiastic applause. Zarnoff had read their minds!

"Thank you so much, ladies and gentlemen. You see, mentalism does work, especially when we're all having so much fun!"

More applause.

*I* was thinking of eighty six. But that's the seventh or eighth number trick in a row. There must be some law, some mathematical tricks he's using. Wait! We've forgotten that he conditions the choice by supposedly guiding our thoughts. If both numbers have to be even, that limits the first digit to six or eight, between the limits of 50 and 100. Then, if the other digit has to be different yet even; we've got only . . . let's see . . . 62, 64, 68 . . . 82, 84, and 86. The 68 and 86 occur twice, so the odds are higher. Actually then, there are six chances he'll be right, but two of them are the same, 68 and 86. He takes that chance with those odds, and enough people in a packed house respond, and Zarnoff comes off the mentalist!

Sure, he's interesting. I applauded, but maybe my applause is for the free ticket, for Cally's sureness that I would be intrigued. She's very dear: her call to me that she'd purchased the ticket for my free night between lectures here in Washington. My gal Thursday!

What's Zarnoff doing now? He's got that person standing up in the tenth row . . .

"Thank you sir. You're initials are indeed 'R.M.'?"

With the corroboration from the stout man about to share his life with the mentalist, Zarnoff wrote some quick notes on a clip-board and pad he held in his hand. His free hand, when not writing, waved gracefully in the air, punctuating the showman thrusts of his resonant voice.

"We've never met, of course. Thank you. Now concentrate on your birthday please. Thank you . . . is it . . . I get a '13' . . . Correct . . . I get 'March 13 . . . 19 . . . 1927'. Are we together tonight?"

The man corroborated every syllable Zarnoff spoke, and the audience applauded energetically.

Zarnoff went on with the man's address, telephone number, and the name of his wife. Next, he asked the man to take out the first bill from his wallet, and he was able to read the serial number perfectly.

That's the old clip-board routine. Old . . . but he handles it beautifully. It amazes me that that man in the audience doesn't recall the survey that was taken in front of the box office: that information he's getting back from Zarnoff was gathered by some assistant posing as a pollster from some local organization. Yep! Written on the clip-board, with copies to Zarnoff. And that assistant had even a keen eye, and so did the cashier: giving him his change with the top one dollar bill serial number controlled. He'd put the change right back into his wallet in the order received, since the bills were in order, and never thought another thing about it. If he had bought popcorn or something . . . no . . . the odds are with Zarnoff again: he does the clip board routine before any intermission, and if the man had pulled out a five . . . Zarnoff could've gotten out of it with a quip . . . something like 'my mind can't think that high' or something. He's good, really good.

He's an obvious Virgo: those big pictures in the lobby give that away, with his eye tiny and piercing, so close together, the smallish features, the tight slightly curly hair. Then the numbers that permeate his act, all the mentalism charade. Sun-Neptune conjuction? That would put his birth in the '30's. Let's see, he's about thirty-seven years old . . . ha! two digits, both odd! . . . looks like Sagittarian Ascendant: the showmanship, the tall figure, those thrusting gestures and . . . and the enthusiasm. That's the real massage for his message. He digs the response out of the audience . . . *and* me!

"And now, friends, I'll need two assistants from the audience."

Zarnoff walked forward on the stage and chose at random three spectators from among the hundreds of hands pumping into the air for recognition.

That would put his birth just before noon. The Mercury would have to be in Virgo as well: Sun-Mercury-Neptune conjunction in Virgo at the Midheaven. Right, the Sagittarian Ascendant. The Moon would have to be in Leo or Sagittarius; it would square that Xth House group from the Ascendant if it were Sagittarius. In Leo, it would be in the VIIIth or IXth, both too weak for him. It's got to be Sagittarius in the Ascendant, the do-your-own-thing Moon. And that's sure what he's doing!

"Thank you. Now, my friends . . . well, I better not say that too soon! We've never met, have we? . . . and we are not friends, correct?"

The audience loved the foolery.

Zarnoff neatly placed the two assistants side by side facing the public, and a stage assistant brought out a small table with a telephone resting on a large telephone book, the cord of the telephone trailing off stage. In the same moment, Zarnoff produced a deck of playing cards out of the air, showed the deck to the assistants, and dramatically asked one of them, a tiny woman in her fifties, wearing a near green suit, to pick a card. He instructed her to hold it securely and tightly after noting its face. She was not to show it to anyone.

Zarnoff then took the telephone book off the table and gave it to the second assistant. He then turned and spoke to the audience.

"The Washington D. C. telephone book here . . . correct, sir? . . . has about 300 pages or so. Now, you there in the third row, think of any number, any number at all between 1 and 300. And you there, yes, you in the red sport jacket, you think of any number at all, similarly. All right now, what are your numbers? Good. We have 265, and yours, sir? You have 178. Now, do you wish to change your numbers?"

The man in the sport jacket made a change. He offered 86, and Zarnoff brought the house down with his quick reply, "Sir, you're several tricks behind us!"

Zarnoff proceeded rapidly, not allowing any possibility of number tampering.

"We have the famous 86 and we have 265. Let's average them, just to show I'm being fair! Madame, will you average 86 and 265, please?"

A young girl in a bright floral blouse blushed and giggled since nobody in the theatre could concentrate on the arithmetic Zarnoff asked for. Again, he handled this beautifully: an assistant suddenly wheeled a blackboard out onto the stage.

"This always happens—especially just before income tax month . . . . . . especially here in Washington!"

The audience was roaring. Zarnoff put the numbers on the board and quickly averaged them to 175.5. Going back to the young lady, he asked, "How should we round it off; up or down?"

The voice squealed out, "Up!" and Zarnoff was eloquent and gracious to the extreme for this young lady's great mathematical contribution, again inviting the applause of the audience.

"You still remember your card, madame? You still have it with you?"

The assistant in the green suit was caught unprepared, since she was totally absorbed in the fun out in the audience. She gulped to attention, checked her card held tightly against her bosom, and nodded complete corroboration to Zarnoff's questions.

Zarnoff suddenly changed the entire mood to seriousness. By just the stillness of his body, a slight lowering of lights that occurred on cue, the audience was hushed.

To the second stage assistant, an accountant type man near sixty, Zarnoff said: "Now sir, please look on page 176 in that telephone directory. You have it? Fine. Now pick a column, and run your finger down to any number you wish. Be sure it is a *personal* number, not a corporation, because we do want someone to answer when we call them!"

The direction of the trick was now totally clear. The assistant confirmed that he had selected the number. Zarnoff took the receiver off the phone, obviously listened briefly for the dial tone, walked with the receiver away from the assistant and the table, stretching the spiral phone cord to its maximum, and instructed the assistant to press the buttons of the number to put the call through.

Another established trick. The old magic books call them "Old Wine". They do mellow in the hands of someone like Zarnoff. It's beautiful how he routines it all. If he were born just before noon with a Sagittarius Ascendant, Aquarius would probably be on his third cusp. That fits. Uranus would probably be in mid-Taurus, trine the Xth House group; he must be 37 years old, born in 1937. Now it's March 1974; Mars is in Gemini. If he's 37, an odd numbered year for him, he would be having his Mars return next year, with Mars' two-year cycle. So now in '74, right now in Gemini, this would suggest that his natal Mars is Sagittarius or at least near there. Gosh, he'd have Mars conjunct the Moon in Sagittarius, the two square that Neptunian Xth House group! It would work. All that showmanship . . . And Saturn in 1937 . . . was . . . uh

. . . was in late Pisces, early Aries. It's got to be early Aries, to strengthen the ego. And that would trine Pluto in late Cancer. Pluto would be in the VIIIth. It all starts to fit . . . and it's wearing out *my* mentalism!

"Sir . . . you've dialed . . . and . . . yes, there it is, I hear the ringing." Zarnoff walked rapidly to the assistant while speaking these words, handing him the phone, and then quickly walked away.

"Be polite now!"

The audience laughed once again, realizing the assistant had no idea yet what to say.

As an apparent after-thought, Zarnoff directed: "Tell the party to hold the line for a moment."

The assistant's voice could be heard faintly: "Uh . . . hello . . . we're calling you from the stage at Kennedy Center. Would you hold the line for a moment . . . please?"

Zarnoff directed the assistant further: "Explain that we're doing a magic show and want the person's cooperation. Ask them to name a card . . . any card . . . a card they feel in the air."

The assistant, showing incredulity and embarrassed reluctance, said just those facts to the person on the other end of the line. Stammering, he concluded, "And would you just name any card for us please . . . any card at all . . . uh, pick it out of the air." There was a long pause. "I know it's late, madame, and you're kind to . . . put up with this. Yes, it is for real. Please just name a card, any card. Thank you."

Zarnoff motioned for the assistant to hang up the telephone, and in the same moment commanded the assistant to name the card, urging him to use his loudest voice.

The assistant gave his best try, his voice grating from the excitement of the experiment: "She said the EIGHT OF HEARTS."

Zarnoff literally flew across the stage to the assistant in the green suit and lifted her hand holding the card high into the air, turning her wrist so that the audience could see the EIGHT OF HEARTS!

Enormous applause roared through the theatre. Zarnoff thanked the assistants and ushered them back to the steps to the audience.

A marvelous trick. Simply marvelous. All the misdirection about the numbers that don't mean anything. I always wonder who is on the other end of the line, kept open by a previous call to that someone and their not hanging up. Zarnoff forced the card beautifully to fit the prearranged choice, and boy! he handled the call expertly, pretending to check the dial tone out himself since the assistant would have detected the direct connection without even dialing. The dial tone maneuver is the only key—keeping the assistant from noting its absence—and Zarnoff handled it superbly.

But, you know, you begin to wonder with all these simple principles put together to form great feats of trickery, masked as pure magic: is everything a trick? Do we trick ourselves in astrology by just focusing enormous perception talents onto something other than ourselves. Getting ourselves out of the way really does the trick. Zarnoff *is* out of the way; he's totally identified with what he's doing. So am I. Then, do we just transcend the mechanics by identifying with them, just as we don't consciously worry about our hearts beating or our lungs inflating? It's style . . . that's what it is . . . personal style, an art, a manner of presentation of the thought process.

I like this man. Everybody seems to. He's here tonight, gone tomorrow. His whole life is planned for jolting sensibilities and moving on. There's the Sagittarius thrust again. Jupiter right now is in late Aquarius. He's got to be 37; that makes his natal Jupiter three cycles of twelve years, plus one Sign back; that's Capricorn. His Jupiter is surely in Capricorn, putting it in his IInd House . . . and that would trine his Xth House group! . . . and his Uranus! He's loaded, and it shows! OK, Mr. Z, I'll bet you you're born in late August or early September 1937, just before noon sometime . . . I better add, Standard Time.

"And now ladies and gentlemen, let's pause for a moment."

The stage lights dimmed, the follow spot brightened, and the blue background effect again dominated the scene.

"I'm getting another mental impression from the audience. I'm getting initials . . . yes, and I'm getting very powerful, concentrated thoughts . . . the person is thinking about me!"

Zarnoff had no clip-board. One hand was poised outstretched to the audience and the other was held to his brow.

"I get the initials 'M. M.' Distinctly. That's correct, 'M. M.' It's a man, and he's thinking about me very intently . . ."

My gosh, that's me. Did Cally set this up? I wasn't in on the survey; I've spoken to no one. He has no clipboard. I'm too far away for him to recognize me; my picture was in the paper yesterday. Maybe an assistant saw me come in and tipped him off. . . . That must be it.

"Will the gentleman M. M. please stand up?"

Zarnoff shielded his eyes from the spotlight and searched the audience. The house lights came up a bit, and the audience rustled in their seats looking about the hall for whoever M. M. was.

Four people stood up from positions to the sides of the hall.

What the hell, I'll stand up too.

Zarnoff waved back into their seats the people to the sides, saying "I get the vibration from the back middle of the orchestra seats. Sir, yes; it is you. Thank you for standing."

He's pointing right at me. Everyone's looking. Well, I'll play along.

"You have the initials 'M. M.'?"

"Yes, I do."

"Ahah! I know you are accustomed to public speaking. Your voice is forthright and strong."

"Thank you. I am."

"Are you from outer space?"

The audience guffawed strongly.

It *is* a set-up. He knows. "Well, no I am not. But

I think you ... uh ... 'pick up' that I work with the planets and the stars."

The audience gasped amazement, but Zarnoff graciously broke the hammy spell: "Ladies and gentlemen, this is no real feat. I simply want to introduce you to Michael Mercury, the famous astrologer, who is in town for a series of lectures."

Damn nice of him, in a way. Maybe Cally did arrange it. She never ceases to amaze me.

It was 9:05. Intermission. I made my way quickly into the lobby, down those red steps, further along the hall, into the Corridor of Nations, and headed to the telephone. Cally's voice was cheery. She *had* set it up and thought she deserved a raise for the effort! She helped me nail down my thoughts about Zarnoff's horoscope. I had been right: he had to have been born September 12 or 13, 1937. Sun, Neptune, and Mercury were in triple conjunction in Virgo, squared by the Moon and Mars in Sagittarius. Saturn was in Aries, trining Pluto. Uranus was in Taurus and was squared by Venus in Leo. My deductions had been a pretty remarkable mentalistic feat in themselves! But in the end, the process of deduction was really the *art* of the discipline.

I thanked Cally profusely and, directed by an usher, made my way further down the immensely tall Kennedy Center corridor with the flags of all the nations of the world creating a cathedral arch of color. I headed for the back-stage entrance, gave my name to the guard, and was quickly ushered into Zarnoff's dressing room.

"Mr. Mercury, how nice to meet you. Thank you for coming back so quickly."

"Thank *you*, Mr. Zarnoff. That was professionally very nice of you . . . the introduction, I mean."

"It's Arthur. Call me Art, please."

"Thanks. I'm Merk. It's a wonderful show!"

"But surely you know many of these principles; you undoubtedly had magic as a hobby as a young man."

Zarnoff was right. I had followed magic and magicians for years as a teenager and in college. This man was imposing. In person in close quarters, his vibration was powerful, charismatic.

"You're right. But your skill is beautiful. You've created illusion . . . with grace."

"Thank you, Merk. But tell me, do you still do some tricks of your own? Some 'mental feats'?"

"In a way, yes." I then summoned some of my teenage showmanship and participated in the spirit of the evening: "How about this? From watching you this evening, I place your birth in 1937, in September. I get the distinct impression of September 12 or 13."

Zarnoff was charitable at my faint imitation of his stage act, even to the hand I raised to my brow.

"You're right! It was September 12. But—and now I'm giving you the typical squelch line I have to live with —you could have gotten that from my publicity somewhere. It might even be printed in the program. You could have made a telephone call before coming backstage!"

"You've got me part way! I figured it out in my head; didn't even look at the program; but I did have my secretary check me out. I called her just before coming to see you.    But, wait a minute. One more thing: were you born just before noon?"

"Touché, Mr. double-M. I was! I was indeed."

Art Zarnoff's demeanor became suddenly serious. His eyes fastened on me tightly. His mind seemed to go into a special gear, and I could feel its vibration.

Zarnoff continued dryly: "OK. How'd you do it? What gave it away?"

"It's just practiced astrological deduction. Certain deductions about character suggest certain symbolisms and their patterns, and the time can be deduced by adjusting those patterns to the 24-hour rotation of the earth, the horizon."

Zarnoff was still serious. "Now that kind of deduction can really be called a trick, couldn't it?"

"Sure. But that's stretching 'trick' pretty far. It's really just . . . just refined technique."

"So's what I do," he said dead seriously.

"*I'll* say! You do it beautifully." I was hoping Zarnoff would release his preoccupation. His mind was still riveted upon me. I could feel it.

"But you know, such tricks—such technique, deductions, knowledge of human behavior—all that works perfectly well *in retrospect*. We can divine what's already happened from clues that range from the infinitesimal to to the blatantly obvious. And we can *anticipate* behavior because of the constancy of past deductions."

"Right. I'll buy that. Astrologers study the past and get corroboration for just that purpose."

"What purpose?"

"Providing a base for the future."

"Aha! There you have it Merk!" Zarnoff finally swirled around as if giving a cape furl around his body. He studied his face in his dressing table mirror, blotted some perspiration from his brow, and then turned back to me. "Tricky technique only holds up when it goes into the past, as I said. There, we can always make adjustments. It can't work *into the future*."

I didn't know where he was going with his discussion. I remained silent.

Zarnoff continued: "I know of no trick—absolutely no trick for going forward into the future. Somebody has always got to . . . 'to take a card' first."

I managed to start a reply, "And yet . . ."

"It works." Zarnoff finished my sentence for me.

"That's precisely what I was going to say. It works. But then again, perhaps helped out by the tiny antennae of observation and feeling that we don't know about, tucked in with our formalized techniques."

"Perhaps. But there is the concept of *time*."

Zarnoff relaxed finally. He half sat on his table and consciously put me at ease. This was a formidable man.

He continued: "You know? I do this work sometimes five times a week. I'm constantly at it with TV shows, radio shows, stage productions, benefits. And, sometimes—mind you, sometimes *there is no trick*! I get ideas, messages. The technique becomes for me to censor them, to keep them *out*." He threw his towel behind him onto the table. "I can tell you, *the future is not entertainment!*"

"You mean it doesn't have the corroboration needed to conclude its . . . its divination."

"Right. The people won't buy it as mentalist entertainment. It sells newspapers if there's disaster and negativism thrown in, and it might unlock the poison in some gypsies' fortune-telling souls, but it doesn't . . . it doesn't please or help the public."

"I see what you mean now, Art. The trick is within the subject then. We get wish fulfillment and expectation all tied up with . . . with motivation or even depression. Fate denies free will; the human focus gets lost."

"Well, that's *your* field, not mine. My point is that you're a good man to come back. I guess I wanted to meet you for some reason I don't understand. I don't usually extend such . . . professional kindnesses, introducing every Tom, Dick, or . . . Michael!" Zarnoff was smiling warmly.

"How did you know I . . . the Mr. 'M. M.' was thinking about you? I mean you didn't have to phrase it that way at all."

"You were. I felt it."

"I was. I was thinking through your horoscope."

"Using *your* techniques?"

"Right. About your present and past."

"Well, what about my future?" Zarnoff opened his arms in jest, but his eyes were still in seriousness.

"Now that's the line *I* live with! I'll turn the tables on you: what about mine?"

Zarnoff didn't move a muscle. His arms were still spread, and his eyes did not blink. He spoke quietly and dryly: "When you come back from the Middle East . . . from . . . from Judea, please be careful of taxicabs."

I almost wanted to laugh, but Zarnoff's hold on me maintained the seriousness of our conversation. I managed to speak smoothly, "Thank you, I will. Anything more? . . . you see, I can't give any corroboration!"

"It's not entertainment. I'm trying to be *helpful*."

"Right. I know you are."

"But I can just say that your world of questions will be answered soon. That time has come."

Zarnoff's last phrase eerily recalled Kali Yuga's first words to me in 1969. The past was recalled and projected into the future. Zarnoff broke the spell and offered his hand and his smile.

"Thank you, Art. What a thrill! I'm really looking forward to the second half."

"Thanks again for coming back. We've met, and that is good. I don't have to wish you the best for your lecture tomorrow. It'll be most successful."

I left the dressing room quickly, and I rushed along the long lobby to the other end of the theatre to get into my seat. The lights were dimming as a signal that intermission was over.

What did he pick up? My name, "Mercury" . . . travel, taxis? No, no . . . he's more sophisticated than that. But that thought in itself always plays right into the hands of the mentalist. The simple details say so much *because* we ordinarily overlook them! . . . But the Middle East! I've got no plans . . . oh well, an amazing man. What's that?! A puff of smoke on the stage! There he is! The trapdoor. Of course! It's old; it works. It's more than a trick; it's technique. I'll applaud Art's technique any day!

*Atlantia curled up her body as before . . .*

## Chapter Nine

### CASE OF THE REGRESSED IDENTITY

Our tables were reserved at the I Ching Asian Restaurant, and Ralph and I got quick service. While we were drinking our soup, Ralph observed: "Merk, that woman at the next table is looking us over; I think she's giving you a wanton look!"

I practically spilled my soup at his pun: "Oh, come on, she recognizes one or both of us, that's all. Either she needs the services of the astrologer Michael Mercury with his world-famous unusual cases or she needs hypnotist Dr. Ralph Stare with his unusually famed other-world cases . . . one or the other . . . that's gotta be it!"

We both laughed at our silliness. We were there to talk business, and the ogler across the way had helped us break the ice.

"Merk, I really think this is a case for you to help out with. I've got this writer, Atlantia Lemoor, who insists on regression hypnosis, but she wants to be able to *prove* it to herself in a way that's never been done before . . . tape-recorders, even film alone won't do . . ."

"But how else can you 'prove' it?"

"That's where you come in. I've been thinking about this for two weeks, and you know how much faith I have in astrology. What if I take her back, really back, in a deep trance, so deep that I can keep out interferences of life experience and residual memory catharsis . . . take her back to the moment of a previous birth . . . to the exact moment . . . sort of in-between lives, at the moment when one identity is aware of taking on the next identity. This awareness would guarantee accuracy of birth-time record."

"That's fantastic, Ralph!" I was stunned. What an idea!

"You'd be with us and, as soon as we established place and time, you'd go to work. You'd probably need more time than I could keep her under, so we'd adjourn. I'd fix the exact moment in her subconscious so we could go right back to it in the next session, and in the meantime, you could make predictions about her previous life personality, the major events in her life etc. Could you do it? Do you think it's valid?"

"Could I do it???" I practically shouted . . . and the woman was staring disapprovingly this time. "Of course I could do it. Ralph, you've got the most exciting idea that's been around in a long time. We could record the horoscope analysis on tape and film, with control witnesses, without the subject of course ... this, uh, Lemoor ... and then in the next session you could see her through the life, and we could make corresponding notes to compare with the horoscope. Wow!"

"I know what you're thinking, Merk: it would prove a lot about astrology and give my client what she's after, this new angle in regression experience."

We finished our courses, talking heatedly about details, about the controls, and found a series of dates when we both would be free to conduct the experiment. I would meet Atlantia Lemoor and Ralph the next morning at 9:00 in his office.

I arrived at the Dakota just before nine. It seemed a perfect day for our experiment: cloudy, the air thick with urban depression. Such an environment would drive anyone back, away from this life. I found my way to the east wing. The plush elevator took me immediately to the third floor, and the receptionist cautioned me to be as quiet as possible.

Ralph met me in the anteroom. He practically whispered: "Good, you're on time. Now listen: I've already begun. I thought it best to put Atlantia into trance before you and the control judges arrived. I filmed and recorded us and also the arrival of the judges when they assembled."

"But, Ralph, you need a control at the hypnotization moment. People could say you planted the date with her!"

"No. Don't worry about that. I've got a special control nurse with me for the experiment. She's also a hypnotist, and she's watching over the whole experiment.

She's much better than some bank-appointed control expert. I wanted Atlantia to be as calm as possible. Don't worry; everything *is* under control."

We went into the inner office very quietly. It was hard to adjust to the darkness. Only pin-point lights lit certain areas of the room: there were the three judges, sitting very solemnly on leather chairs at the foot of the couch. The nurse sat above the couch just behind Atlantia's head. Atlantia herself appeared to be sleeping peacefully. She was about 42, Neptunian face, full lips, black hair, dark-blue, loose-fitting, fine tweed pants-suit. I noticed that she wore no jewelry, no make-up . . . not even a wristwatch. She was serene and simple. She had to be a Pisces.

An Ekron 2000A-4 camera was mounted on the bookcase above the couch. This camera was well-known in the field: it had a super-sensitive film and lens complex that allowed fine realization record with minimum light. Ralph used a black-light process that we could see only as a faint gray aura around the couch, including the nurse and Ralph's chair beside Atlantia.

I nodded to the judges and to the nurse, and Ralph motioned that I should sit in his chair. He sat on the edge of the couch at the level of Atlantia's waist. He sat in silence for a few moments, checking Atlantia's pulse and random eye movements. The room became absolutely still. He lifted his hand to an electric eye control shining in the bookcase. The slight sound that followed told us that the sound film camera and tape recorder were in operation. I then saw the microphones . . . two of them, also in the bookcase, about 18 inches above Atlantia's head and just the slightest bit behind her. Ralph began to speak to her, and I took out my pad and flashlight pencil.

"Now, Atlantia, we are leaving the present, we are leaving your name, your birth in this life . . . leaving, leaving, going back . . . back . . . back to wherever the spirits of time will lead you." Ralph's voice was beautiful, restful, authoritative, while still protective. "Pass your lifetimes by, Atlantia, let them fall away from the entrance to the past . . . the wheat separates for you . . . opens before you . . . a sea divided . . . you enter deep into the worlds gone by . . . deep . . . deep . . . as far back toward a distant Sun as you care to go. It's beautiful, beautiful, way off there . . . walk to the Sun, reach for it and take your place again in life, sometime, somewhere, someone. You are becoming someone else . . . a life, a life you've lived before beyond the fields of wheat blown by the winds of time . . . a life you've lived before . . . share with us, whisper to us the song of that birth . . . share with us that moment of birth, that time and place . . . find it, dear soul, find it, embrace it, share it with us . . . we are waiting . . . waiting . . . reach for the Sun, make it yours . . . share the moment with us . . . we are waiting . . ."

Ralph's voice trailed off. Atlantia's face showed slight tremors around her mouth and eyes. It was as if her eyes were open and glowing underneath her closed lids. Her hands came together to her chest. She rolled slightly to her side. Ralph went to his knees on the floor so as not to disturb her natural motion . . . her fetal movement. We were so close . . . "Find it, dear soul . . . tell us, whisper, whisper . . . where are you? Where are you . . .?"

Atlantia's voice came through unmoving lips . . . a dark sound, slurred, almost foreign in tone . . . "Magdala . . . Magdala . . . water . . . the sea . . . Magdala . . ."

"Where is Magdala, where is Magdala . . . is it beautiful, are you comfortable . . .?" Ralph urged her so delicately.

"Yes . . . yes . . . Magdala . . . Sea . . . of . . . Sea of Galilee . . . I'm coming to Magdala . . . Father Phillip . . . to Phillip . . ."

I wrote "Magdala, Sea of Galilee" on my pad.

Ralph resumed: "What year is it, oh soul? What year is it . . . please share the moment with us . . . please. You are in Magdala . . . Father Phillip is waiting . . . what year is it?"

Atlantia whispered, almost singing quietly in the lilt of the words: a low dark tone with pronounced nasal resonance, "The Law of Herod, Great Herod . . . ended twelve years ago . . . twelve ago . . . now twelve years with son . . . Antipas twelve . . ." I wrote carefully.

Ralph urged her further: "Thank you, oh soul, now when in Antipas twelve . . . when? What time of day or night is it? What day . . . what *day* is it . . . when does this miracle take place . . . please share it with us."

". . . in . . . in . . . the month of Thamus . . . Thamus . . . five days before the full light of sister Moon . . . Child to Sun . . . Thamus . . . sunrise in Magdala . . . for father Phillip . . . festival . . . temple joy . . . Jews feast the birth . . ." Her voice faded.

"Thank you, dear spirit, and welcome! . . . welcome to life . . . we will let you rest now . . . but remember . . . always remember . . . we will live the life soon again . . ."

"No, NO!" broke in Atlantia's voice, "she can not, *should* not . . ."

Ralph without alarm soothed her: "We agree . . . please understand . . . we will live the life again *in memory* . . . in memory only . . . we will return to this life . . . remember the place Magdala, the time . . . we will return to learn what 'she' did," and Ralph glanced at me quickly, "now come back from that Sun, through the fields of wheat . . . come back to us here, through ages of time . . . come back slowly and beautifully, remembering only the year, date and time long ago . . . come back and rest with us here . . . sleep in 1975 . . . nine-teen-seventy-five. Find us and rest . . . sleep . . . peace, peacefully . . ."

Ralph raised his hand again to the electric eye, stopping tape and camera. He motioned for the nurse to take over pulse-check and the hypnotic rest period. Ralph brought us all—the judges and me—into his anteroom. The judges spoke first, all together, most enthusiastically: "Congratulations, Doctor Stare . . . exemplary . . . superb."

"Not yet, gentlemen. Tomorrow we will see. Nine AM again as we planned?" The judges agreed, we all shook hands . . . they, a bit incredulously, and they left Ralph and me alone.

"I'm exhausted, Merk." Ralph sat down heavily.

"That was beautifully done. I think we have it ...no need to check the tape: Magdala, the Sea of Galilee...and references to Herod's reign and the other conversation...I got it all clearly, but I must study it. I've left the whole day open for this. I'll call if I do need the replay."

"Remember she said 'she' at the end...it must be a woman."

"Right. That will help, of course."

I left quickly. I knew Ralph needed a rest, and he still had to revive Atlantia. And I needed to do lots of research to erect the horoscope.

I briefed Cally and sent her to the library. I had had an idea in the cab. Now I had to check it out. I took down from my library shelves the *Dictionary of the Bible*, the *Atlas of the Ancient World*, the *Bible* itself, and some Kabbalistic books. I first studied the maps: in the time of Herod the Great, almost all of what is now Israel... then called Samaria...was under his rule, including the Sea of Galilee. Magdala was right on the Sea's western shore at 35 East 30, 32 North 40. The *Dictionary* told me that Herod the Great had died in 4 B.C., and that the kingdom was divided among his three sons: Archelaus became king of Judea; Herod Antipas became tetrarch of Galilee and Perea; and Phillip became tetrarch of Ituraea and ... 'Phillip'! I switched to my notes: Atlantia had said 'I'm coming to Magdala . . . Father Phillip . . . to Phillip.' She was born 'the Law of Herod, Great

Herod ended twelve years ago.' . . . that would be her birth year: 8 A.D. . . . her father was Phillip, son of Herod the Great.

I checked further: she was born in Galilee, ruled by the other son, Herod Antipas, brother of Phillip . . . 'Antipas twelve' . . . It checked: she was born in 8 A.D., twelve years after Herod the Great had died, twelve years into Antipas's reign. She was born to Herod Antipas's brother, Phillip.

My idea came back to me . . . the one I had had in the cab: I searched the *Dictionary* index on my hunch, then the *Bible*: Matthew 14:3-11, Mark 6:17-28. I was right!! The daughter of Phillip, brother of Herod, was Salome . . . Salome!! Chills ran through me. It was overwhelming: we had *seen* Salome's birth not two hours ago!

The time, the date: in the month of Thamus . . . my Kabbala book said this was the Hebrew month of July . . . Atlantia had said 'sunrise in Magdala, five days before the full light of sister Moon . . . child to Sun, sister to Moon . . .' When was the Full Moon in July in 8 A.D.? What a question! I searched my records, but nothing was that precise. Then I called my teacher, Mr. Clyptic; he'd be able to help.

Clyptic and I talked for about 30 minutes. He got out some of his ancient texts. One by Rabbi Muri-Kalagav-Shamum listed the lunations between Passovers from 37 B.C., Herod's taking of Jerusalem, to the naming of Caligula emperor at Passover in 37 A.D. Clyptic made the calendar corrections for me while we were on the phone, then he said there was no doubt about it: the Full Moon came at Sidereal Time 8-10-39, within a margin of one hour either way. We computed that that date represented July 25.

I put my information together. It's incredible that Salome had popped into my mind in the cab ride home. We were understandably hyper-elevated, and somehow I had picked up a vibration with *her* name on it! Incredible. Salome had been born on July 25, at sunrise, in 8 A.D. on the Sea of Galilee.

Cally had returned during my phone conversation with Clyptic and laid the books on my desk: Oscar Wilde's play and Richard Strauss's opera score, both entitled *Salome*. I explained what I had discovered to her, and she too was overwhelmed.

Now we had the tedious work of calculating the planet positions back to that date. We could be reasonably sure with the heavy planets and, thanks to Atlantia ... Salome ... to the relative position of Sun and Moon. We kept at it and made cross references to known horoscopes back through the ages to check. After two hours, we were pretty sure.

Clyptic called me back. He too was fascinated at pinpointing the positions and, in reading further in his very old texts, had discovered a reference to Venus at that time. He read it to me, in translation: "The light of Azrael and its spirit Araziel shone in evening song in the first part of Schaltiel, in the Summer feast of Hezion's offspring gathered together north and south, one month past the longest day." This was complicated ... in the

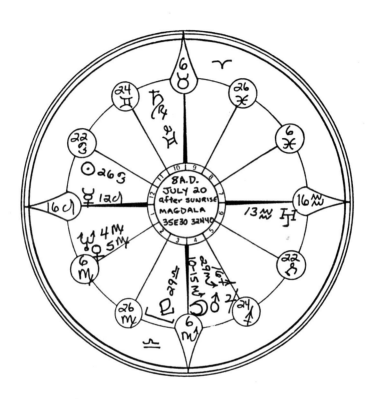

almost codified style of the ancient Jewish scribes . . .
but we figured it out: the passage referred to a Venus
Hesperus, with longitude greater than the Sun, in the
first third or first half of Virgo . . . in July, in 8 A.D.
when Judea and Samaria were incorporated with the
province of Syria, ruled by descendants from Hezion.
We could be relatively sure of Venus in 1 to 5 Virgo.
This was vitally important as I inspected the horoscope,
now complete. I had placed Mercury on the horizon
until I could "feel" rectification clarification. And I placed
Mars arbitrarily in the IVth. This would surely check
out along with Saturn, the father-mother situation in
Salome's life. I knew about her and St. John the Baptist,
of course . . . and I also knew from Matthew and Mark
that she was the daughter of Phillip and Herodias, and
that Herod then arranged to marry his living brother's
wife, forcibly and dramatically against the ethical laws
of the day. Herodias had herself seemingly engineered
this drastic maneuver. What a woman she must have
been! And Salome was caught in the middle!

Salome was definitely a Cancer with a Leo Ascendant . . . "Child to Sun, Sister to Moon." All the measurements checked to a reasonable margin of error. I spent
the next two hours reading Wilde's play and the English
and German texts that accompanied Strauss's opera.
In the first pages, I was astonished. The very first lines
compared Salome to the Moon: "How strange the moon
seems . . . she's like a woman rising from a tomb . . .
Salome is very fair, pale, pale . . . shadow of a snow-
white rose in a mirror of silver . . . you must not look at
her . . . terrible things may happen."

When Salome appears, she says the same things: "How good it is to see the moon. She is like a silver flower, cold and chaste. I am quite sure she is a Virgin; she has a Virgin's beauty ..." It was uncanny that Wilde and Strauss, in their artistic sensitivities divined that *this was* the Salome complex: the "passionate virgin." In the horoscope, there it was: Venus in Virgo and Neptune in close conjunction in Virgo in the First House, squared by retrograde Saturn in the Xth, definitely sextiled by the Moon in Scorpio ... and probably Mars, both in the IVth ... the XIIth House Sun squared by Pluto in Libra. I made notes on my typewriter.

When Herod himself appears in the opera and play he too comments on the Moon: "It looketh strange tonight, like a mad woman! ..." and at the end he calls to her servants ... during the orgy with the Head of St. John ... to "hide the moon, hide the stars, something terrible will come!" AND THE MOON DISAPPEARS. Then, Herod orders Salome crushed under the soldiers' shields for her horrible lust and depravity. There must have been something phenomenal about the Moon on the night St. John and Salome died. Or maybe this was just dramatic symbology, artistic convenience on Wilde's and Strauss's parts. I had to check ... just maybe ...

References pin-point John's murder in 29 A.D. in the month of Ab or Lous, the two words for August, at the birthday feast of Herod. I called Clyptic again, and for a full hour on the phone he searched the Kalagav-Shamum text for that month or for a phenomenon then in the heavens. And there it was: "The spirit Gaphiel was punished by Michael and given new life in Phakiel's home after the sins of the day for the meaning for tomorrow, for that Ab and the Abs to follow". The Moon had been "punished by the Sun!" and given new life in the memory of that day . . . in mid Leo . . . conjunct Salome's Ascendant . . . *an eclipse*. It fits!

Salome would have been 21 at that time, older than the usual text commentaries had her. Transit Saturn would have been in the last square to its birth position from near the VIIIth cusp. The progressed Sun would have been conjunct the Ascendant with the progressed Moon . . . with the transit eclipse one month after her birthday. Transiting Uranus, 21 years after birth, would square the Eclipse-Ascendant point from 13 Taurus. The radix Jupiter trines the Ascendant, to be sure, from the IVth . . . and Salome chose the head of Saint John as her *reward* for dancing. Herod had offered her anything in reward . . . any speculation at all would have been rewarded. Her mother, described as so conniving and vicious in early texts, told her to select the head. Here was the Uranus transit, the mother influence . . . the hate for Herod . . . the family shame when John the Baptist had told Herod he had sinned by taking his brother's wife. It was all there in the horoscope . . . if I could just make it clear . . . if Atlantia could corroborate.

I typed up a summary, re-studied it, and sealed it in an envelope. Only I knew what was in that envelope.

The next morning, we all gathered again at Ralph's office. As before, Atlantia was already in a deep trance. The judges, the nurse . . . the same positions in the room. I gave the envelope to the judges. They marked it with their seal and noted the time upon it. Even this exchange was filmed and recorded with a special time device on the film that recorded the actual timing of filming indelibly on the film track.

Ralph told us quietly that, now that the birth time and place had been established in Atlantia's sub-conscious, we could expect a swift entrance into the old life and a free-flowing narrative. He began to take Atlantia back.

I studied her face again . . . and I noted several differences, which seemed not to have attracted notice from anyone else . . . but for me, they practically lifted me out of my chair with eerie excitement: she had long earrings on, and around her neck, a long, fine, silver scarf! It was all very tasteful and natural . . . but in contrast to her plainness the day before . . . in relation to my analysis . . . might her subconscious have dictated this change of appearance?

Atlantia curled up her body as before when she arrived at Magdala and 8 A.D., but then her narrative was swift, poetic and strangely obscure in image . . . but it came out unhaltingly . . . as Ralph had told us to anticipate. When regression is total, the line of communication is often swift and articulate, even from the ancient times of the Middle East.

"Oh, Phillip, kind Phillip, I have come . . . take me to the sea and lands beyond; let us see where He was born, the One who will walk with men and speak of love . . . forget Mother's demand . . . the emperor is new; he loves us . . . Tiberius, Tiberius . . . let us live together . . . together on the Sea . . . Why can't we live together? Why? But father, I wish to remain . . . not to Sepphoris . . . Mother, why must we go with Herod . . . HEROD, no, no, Tetrarch, I am old enough a wife to be, since one year and three . . . NO . . . you have taken my mother, you can not take me from me . . ."

Atlantia became extraordinarily agitated, resistant: "You wish me to hide your secret . . . but not by floods nor by great waters can ever the heat of your passion be thirsted . . . I live a prisoner in my mother's delight, my father's sorrow, and Herod's plan . . . peace this time and I pledge my silence . . .

"Who is that man below in the cistern there? A man called John, what has he done? Is he beautiful? . . . This torment enflames me, it surrounds me within, but I am prisoner too; the pale of weakness stung by the Scorpion of desert's waste . . . I live silently with my mother's blood and the sin of her Tetrarch . . . Am I like her? . . . Has this man below come to accuse us both on the hated birthday of the despised Tetrarch? . . . I see my prisoner now, alabaster white, hair of Cyprus, the eyes of Jokanaan open to darkness yet blind to the strange feelings in my blood . . . in hate and love . . . in pain of life and love, imprisoned freedoms . . . I taunt Tetrarch through the one who has seen the sins . . . I meet the spirit . . . the mystery of love is greater than the deed . . . and so close to the mystery of death . . .

"Now in three-quarter life, I know no man . . . only hate of men but love of desire . . . and the spirit's flight in the dream of day . . . to have the blood-tie freed . . . Dance? Dance? . . . of course, my secret pledge to give for not being taken . . . Dance . . . in the weakness of my swoon, in the prison of my desires . . ."

Atlantia . . . Salome was perspiring, still in high tension . . . "my reward? . . . if only I could say it . . . peacocks and palaces . . . feasts of simple love . . . Phillip returned . . . yet, mother's blood speaks in my heart . . . to defeat the sin . . . the head of the sinners' witness . . . revenge of Herodias, and . . . and freedom for my awakened desire . . . the desire for someone from beyond, from below . . . the head . . . the head . . . Salomaia will kiss the mouth and seal a life that is gone and a new life that is to come."

Atlantia's voice had changed . . . it was maniacal . . . Ralph instantly saw the dangers . . . he soothed her . . . interrupted her thought. The nurse swiftly gave an injection into the back of her hand . . . the tensions left Atlantia's face.

Ralph turned to us and whispered: "Gentlemen, that is all we can do; please come with me."

We went into the anteroom. All of us were silent in shock.

Ralph spoke first: "Gentlemen, I interrupted Miss Lemoor because she was near a crisis, perhaps vivid recall of death. Please understand. But, I'm sure that we have enough here to please us all in the interest of science,

to fulfill the experiment. Before we discuss it, I think
we should read what Mr. Mercury has sealed in that envelope."

The judges opened the envelope and handed each of
us a copy of my analysis:

*From the data supplied by the subject, Atlantia
Lemoor, in the presence of the formal control
group on Tuesday, February 16, 1975, I was
able to ascertain the birth of the personality as
July 25, 8 A.D. in Magdala, on the Sea of Galilee, just after Sunrise.   The Appendix to this report contains all details of computation and
horoscopic deduction.*

*The reference in trance alluded to 'father Phil-
lip.' I submit that the regressed personality will
become, was Salome (Salomaia), daughter of
Phillip and Herodias (Tetrarch of Ituraea and
Trachonitis), son of Herod the Great.*

*The life would be torn apart by the parents,
perhaps in the 7th and 8th years, especially,
when Herod Antipas married his brother Phillip's wife, Herodias . . . at her urging . . . and
took mother and child with him to his walled
metropolis at Sepphoris.*

*Just prior to this, the subject would have en-
joyed travel and unusual exposure through her
father. · This point is conjecture, but the Mercury possibly positioned upon her Ascendant
would point in this direction; expounded in
the Appendix.   She would have resisted the*

*switch in households; her real identity would
have been lost to a new direction.*

*The deep emotional crisis would have developed
in relation to the guilt that she was becoming
like her mother . . . and, quite probably, an at-
tempted rape or sexual opportunizing from her
step-father when she was 17, some four years
past the marrying age at that time.*

*The subject is a fantasized, problematic virginal
personality. Lust and imagination are awakened
crucially at 17 and grow in an imprisoned guilt
of self-awakening and being like her mother,
sharing the same blood, as it were.*

*Mysteries and teaching of all kind abounded
at that time and deeply seeded the subject's
imagination. She was undoubtedly anemic,
pale, weak, and, outwardly, appeared ascetic.
Yet, inside, a deep vague, gnawing passion
veiled in fantasy brought a guilt and fear to
her that were enormous.*

*The crisis of her life would occur shortly after
her 21st year, when an extraordinary eclipse
of the Sun took place on her Ascendant, and
crucial transits and progressions triggered a
dramatic resolution somehow of this emotional complex. This year is corroborated*
historically *as well: the year of Salome's death
after the murder of St. John.*

*The mother's influence is dominant then. The
Venus in the chart is overwhelmingly impor-*

*tant. The subject would be rewarded some-
how, her passion and guilt resolved . . . and,
in that reward, she would cross the line to
eternal sorrow, depression, guilt, and psycho-
logical pain that could only lead to traumatic
death.*

*We know the Salome story in general. But,
to the best of my ability, I have reported the
overall view of the horoscope without incor-
porating the story, as we know it, subjectively.
I refer you to the Appendix for further details
and explanation.*


The judges and Ralph knew the accuracy of what
I had written. Atlantia had corroborated it all, the deepest guilts and emotional pain, the lure of the mysteries
focused in John the Baptist. There was so much to add
now . . . so much that would be more artistic than scientific . . . but none the less valid, really. We all shook
hands. And, with many compliments and arrangements
for the formal impounding of the evidence and panel
review, the judges left.

Ralph and I sat together, and I shared with him
some of the technical details of the horoscope that he
could understand, especially the square between Uranus
and the Scorpio Moon and how the Sun entered this by
Progression at 17.    But one observation in particular
caused us again to sit in silence, in awe of what we had
been through:

"And, Ralph, I do believe that Pluto is Baptism, regeneration, here square to the Sun in Venus' Sign, Libra. That Direction to the IVth cusp triggered the big family switch when Salome was nearly 8 years old. But I keep coming back to the Venus-Neptune in Virgo . . . that is the deep key, with the square from Saturn, of course . . . but nobody except an astrologer can appreciate . . . that Venus rules the dance and Neptune rules the veil!"

## Chapter Ten

### MICHAEL MERCURY - REQUIEM

I know now ... I know ... I've felt it, but I've felt nothing. I see the crash below me ... the collision. Somehow Zarnoff knew. My body is gone. And sorrow: Cally, Stella, Ralph ... the newspaper obituary ... I know all and see all in one moment of awareness. I'm dead, yet somehow I live. I have no form, yet I'm *all* forms. Will I be guarded in peace?

And happy: I'm somehow freed ... somehow prepared for the mysteries. This light around me: a oneness with answer. I am a part of All; my questions find answers before they're asked; my thoughts are the thoughts of time. Is there a God to welcome me, to receive what I tried to be. Was my work true?

"Yes and no " was my answer.

No? What was *not* true?

"True, yes. Complete, no."

The answer intrigued me. Had I assumed that astrology was all? Are there other dimensions operating through astrology? Are there other planets to be discovered that will unify even more what we know already?

"Yes" was my answer.

What about the Star, Ego Redemptionis, that fantastic story I created for Miss Fortunata?

"That too was true," came my answer.

But how could it have been true? I created it out of my imagination.

"Your imagination is the mirror of time's mysteries."

I know . . . at least, I think I do . . . but—

"What has existed, exists yet. What is to come is known now."

Then that Star . . . it does belong to everyman. Everyman's will to become, to overcome, to remember his place in creation.

"The Will is a gift."

And the sharing of destinies, the hope for understanding . . . these too are bonds within time within . . .

"Within the Order."

And it all began with that Yuga case. Somehow I was reborn . . . refreshed, made aware of the possibility . . . that's it! *The possibility* of becoming more than I was then.

"Every man can become more in his moment."

I know, I know. I had faith that I was doing right, that I was working with the true symbols of harmony . . . the harmony within the Order.

"And the Order preserves life."

Of course it does, of course! I see it all now, so clearly: the Order *preserves* life, it doesn't *cause* it. The Order was set beyond time. We just can't . . . couldn't conceive of it. Through his life, man works with the Order, within it, to preserve what must be, not to destroy the harmony, or change it, the geometry. But wouldn't this be Fate?

"No. The Moment of Order is a moment only."

A moment? 'The twinkling of an eye.' Man's time is his own creation. Fate needs duration. But the Moment is . . . it just is. And what was and was to be . . . will be . . . is now . . . ever shall be . . . it's all one Moment! One massive Moment . . . or small moment . . . in a focus of Order! Wow! What a thought! I should have seen that. I should take every client I have . . . had . . . and lift them up . . . suspend them . . . bring the mirror of their own imaginations into operation. I'd ask them, "What do you want to do with your life?" And *they would know!* Somehow they would know . . . because they shared the Moment by being alive within it and the moments to come that exist now. A black tomorrow seems to lose all its painful perspective . . . and a difficult yesterday as well. Maybe that's what Cally did instinctively with that *Casey at the Bat* poem; she read into it the feeling of her own moment, gave the past life in the present. And that's nostalgia. We did that with the Salome regression too. The moments are *all* still there if we just gain awareness of them . . . even this moment of my death . . . or is it my rebirth? Am I to go on again . . . will I be aware of it?

"You will not be aware."

Why not . . . why can *I* not be allowed to be aware? *I* would know how to handle it.

"To give you the benefit of mystery."

The benefit of mystery . . . is that it? Is that what our moment is: the effort to understand, to grow in wisdom and find the way?

"Yes. The Way is Mine."

And man sub-divides the Way . . . just as he does time, the Moment. All the Religions, all the cults, Astrology, I Ching, Palmistry, Psychoanalysis, Witchcraft, the Sciences . . . all work as sub-divisions of the Way to understand the mystery. Was my sub-division, was my work . . . uh . . . worthwhile?

"Indeed it was: you cared."

I *did* care. I thought, I felt, I prayed through the respect I had for the Order. And Einblick did too: he captured an infinitesimal spark of the Moment within his work . . . far larger than he even realized. It's not hard to understand now, really. I see how the part reflecting the whole, the micro-macrocosm theories apply to the extreme, not just to geometric arrangement, but to the time dimensions as well. I must be right.

"You are, to a degree."

To a degree . . . what could be missing . . . perhaps an element of faith. THAT'S it: Faith. I had it. I *believed* in the work I could do with astrology. I didn't believe *in astrology*; I believed in myself. I was perfectly in tune with my position within the Moment. In this harmony, I seemed to have power. Astrology was my discipline, my medium.

"And responsibility."

And responsibility for sure. It's all too easy to dabble in life, in astrology, in religion, in communication of any kind. It's the responsibility factor that grounds the effort, that focuses one human vibration with another within a division of the One Moment. That must be it.

"Yes. Responsibility and love."

Now I see. The love is the essence of our being: it's what every person shares with every other person. The love says: we're both in this Moment together. The two awarenesses create a focus that opens awareness. That's why ice cold predictions don't work in horoscopes ... my losing my hand for example ... that was coincidence, I'm sure ... the glove that was missing. *Predictions are the product of combined awareness.* If something *can be*, the person himself knows it. The future moment already exists: *on* paper and *in* life. The astrologer just awakens the client, lifts him to the level where he *sees* that it can be. That's it. That's what I knew somehow. This love recognizes, illuminates the Way ... and it must have been the love that began the Moment.

"It was."

And Newton, Kepler, Brahe ... so many. These men and the many others, they went just so far with astrology ... they knew so much ... but then they stopped. Somehow their moment *within* the Moment didn't allow the freedom, the individual freedom that allowed love to speak with recognition. Why not? ... why was it that—

"The love is the God within."

Of course!! *Our* Age *allows* it. The Age of Aquarius/ Leo: we're finding in each of us recognition of our own godliness. But why must it all emerge from such disorder and social upset?

"Harmony emerges from dissonance."

That's beyond me. But then again, dissonance is relative to the sophistication, to individual and group perspective within the Moment. What is dissonance in one part of the Moment is harmony in another . . . but these are our terms . . . or are they? What did Yuga mean: New births occur unseen? Maybe we have seen the possibility of harmony many, many, many times in our years of the Moment, and NEVER RECOGNIZED IT! Like a record playing over and over again in the same groove. Are we now ready to replace the tone arm, to make progress?

And the astrologer. What part does he play? Is every astrologer equipped with the love for another's awareness? Or, is it all show and testing on his own part, to prove his control of technique. Lord knows, I cared about Paula Catherine's death . . . at the peak of her life. Maybe that's what brought those symbols to life for me. I did care. *My* moment of caring embraced her *last* moment. I understood somehow, a part of it all.

My life is gone, successors will comfort my grave, and a new age has begun. What will emerge to translate further bloom to man . . . as I . . . as I become one somehow with Time's Way? What is it that binds man to man; what is this love? What is it that gave it life and that urges others to learn, to hope, to know, to help, *to help* and serve in their fullness of time ... what is it that makes astrology live for those who really care to share?

"It is the Creative Principle."

Thank you. Yes! Thank you!

"Mr. Merkurius, you are welcomed."